ADVANCE P

Maribeth Decker uses real life stories about the animals she has helped to debunk the myths about our loyal companions. She explains in easy to digest language how the laws of physics prove that our animals live on. And she shares how we know when it is time to allow our animals to transition. For any animal lover, her words ring true in our own experiences. I felt all of this when we had to say goodbye to our beloved cat Ashley. A fun and enlightening read!

— CHERI D. ANDREWS, ESQ., AUTHOR OF *SMOOTH SAILING: A PRACTICAL GUIDE TO LEGALLY PROTECTING YOUR BUSINESS*

Finally! A much-needed wonderful book to help connect the energy of our beloved pets with our energy and that of our ancestors. If you loved Dr. Brian Weiss' *Many Masters, Many Lives*, you would love this book. And how powerful it is when we realize we're all connected via an energetic internet. Maribeth leads you on a beautiful journey to explore and places words to what you already know in your heart.

— MARA BENNER, FOUR DIRECTIONS WELLNESS, AFFILIATED WITH THE GW CENTER FOR INTEGRATIVE MEDICINE

Are you an animal guardian whose mental reaction at the thought of your pet's passing is freeze and flight? Like you cannot face taking in the fact that this day will inevitably come even for *your* animal friend? Are you experiencing total denial? If so, please give yourself the gift of reading Maribeth Decker's book *Peace in Passing*. She shares her expertise, wisdom, and experience from this field with you, in abundance, and your panic and denial will be replaced with curiosity, understanding, and above all comfort. Thanks, Maribeth!

— HANNE BRØTER, YOUR BRAND VISION: GRAPHIC
DESIGN AND VISUAL BRANDING

Peace in Passing will change your understanding of your relationship with your beloved pets. Maribeth will become your trusted mentor through extremely difficult decisions and transitions.

— KAREN CAMPBELL, OWNED BY SCOTTISH TERRIERS,
AND OWNER OF CAMPBELL'S SCOTTISH TERRIERS

Losing a beloved pet is heartbreaking. You miss your companion, and you are often left with so many questions: Did I do everything for her? Is she mad? Did I let her go too soon? Thankfully, you can help find answers to these questions through Maribeth Decker's amazing book, *Peace in Passing*. What you'll learn in this book will help you make the best decisions for your pet—and help you mourn the loss of your friend. Highly recommended to all pet people!

— JILL CELESTE, AUTHOR, *LOUD WOMAN: GOOD-BYE,*
INNER GOOD GIRL!

The expanded edition of *Peace in Passing* is a true gem. As in the first edition, the author includes many real-life stories of pet guardians who have lost a pet. I can relate to every single story and find knowing that there are other pet guardians out there just like me a source of solace. Maribeth explains the transition process so clearly and compassionately. While it's a blessing that we can help our pets along to the next phase in their journey, the weight of that responsibility is immense. Maribeth understands this and provides a framework to more peacefully navigate the highly emotional process. My two dogs and cats were old, so I was anticipating the end for a while. However, when it comes, it's still a shock. I loved how Maribeth offered ways to plan for the transition. I wish I had done this in a more concrete and specific way but will certainly incorporate Maribeth's approach when it's time to say goodbye again. I deeply appreciated her ability to convey the spiritual nature of the entire process. She helped me recognize the way my departed animals are communicating with me from the other side. She helped me trust these communications and trust my communications to and for them. For any pet guardian who will eventually face the loss of a much-loved family member, I highly encourage you to read these books!

— CYNTHIA DACOSTA, HEART-INSPIRED THERAPEUTIC
COACH AT CYNTHIADACOSTA.COM

Peace in Passing helps pet guardians navigate their animals' transition process. Readers learn how to keep their animals comfortable and to embody love as a powerful healing energy before and during transition. This expanded second edition offers alternative resources for comforting and communicating with animals in this life and the afterlife. It provides a comprehensive introduction for beginners and continuous learning for seasoned animal communicators and energy healers. Medical intuition, quantum versus classical physics, and other topics are explained simply yet thoroughly. Spirits—of pets and wild animals we help—reassure us that they remain present, as our teachers and cherished companions.

— ERIN PATRICIA DOHERTY, INTUITIVE ANIMAL
COMMUNICATOR AND REIKI MASTER,
WRITER/EDITOR, AND PET SITTER

Peace in Passing is a MUST read for everyone who has ever experienced loss of any kind. With the focus on our beloved animals passing, Maribeth beautifully captures the disconnect that is often felt when our animal family passes compared to losses in our human family. This book takes you through the entire process of animal transition, from the timing of death all the way through the thoughts we might experience even years after their passing and choosing a new animal. This book offers us immense peace during transitions themselves. However, what I didn't expect was that *Peace in Passing* creates the space for us to become closer to animals while they are alive. I'm so thrilled that Maribeth's experience and words allow us to experience the joy that our animals bring to our lives on a deeper level now!

— JESSICA DUGAS, THE BREAKTHROUGH
SHOW NETWORK

Peace in Passing begins with easy-to-comprehend modern scientific explanations of the energetic physics of life and passing. It weaves together the importance of our pets to us, ways to communicate with them and listen to their inner thoughts, especially as they near the end of their life. Anyone who is having any doubts about *the right thing to do* or *am I really that close to my pet,* can put those doubts to rest with the information provided in this book and the stories shared. I am appreciative of how clearly presented are the caring final steps we can take to assist our pets, ourselves, and our loved ones. This is an incredible resource for anyone with a pet at any age, so you can be prepared and make the most out of every day with your pet.

— KARIN EDGETT

In *Peace in Passing,* Maribeth Decker provides an important number of ways to help people navigate the hardest time of their lives with their beloved animal companions—knowing the end is approaching. Along with providing powerful mindsets and tools for navigating this last phase of their animal's life, she provides ideas on how to prepare oneself and one's animals for the transition and best practices on how to be fully present during the transition. This book brings addition comfort with heartwarming stories of animals during all phases of their lives. If you are experiencing this kind of transition in your relationship with an animal you love, you are in expert hands with Maribeth and this book.

— FABIENNE FREDRICKSON, AUTHOR OF *EMBRACE YOUR MAGNIFICENCE: GET OUT OF YOUR OWN WAY AND LIVE A RICHER, FULLER, MORE ABUNDANT LIFE*

Peace in Passing is a comprehensive guide to all aspects of the process of a pet's transition from this life. Maribeth Decker debunks societal myths, offers practical strategies for conventional, and alternative therapies to support aging and dying pets, and shares a multitude of true stories that illustrate her lessons in inspiring ways. Her loving approach and supportive voice can be heard throughout the book, gently walking you through this sacred time with your pet. Maribeth answers the questions at the top of your mind and ones that you didn't even know that you had. I highly recommend this book for all animal lovers to help them navigate this challenging time and create a graceful transition for their beloved pet—and themselves.

— DR. CARA GUBBINS, ANIMAL COMMUNICATOR AND
AUTHOR OF *DIVINE BEINGS: THE SPIRITUAL LIVES AND
LESSONS OF ANIMALS*

In this new and expanded second edition of *Peace in Passing*, the author covers trickier topics about the transition of our beloved pets. In this edition, Maribeth writes about her extensive work with animals facing the end of their physical lives. Through the case studies she presents of pets and their humans, we readers become more aware of the options available to us. Maribeth is a comforting, confident guide. She reassures us that our strong connection with our pet can help us make good decisions. This connection along with her shared knowledge and experiences in the book make for a powerful combination.

— LIZ GUTHRIDGE, EXECUTIVE COACH AND ALLIANCE
OF THERAPY DOGS VOLUNTEER

Peace in Passing is a wonderful combination of comfort, stories, wisdom, and advice. Ms. Decker has written a heartfelt book to help you and your pet get through end-of-life transitions as easily as is possible. She addresses all aspects, including before, during, and after. She also shares practical things you can do to help your pet feel the best that they can at any stage in life. As a client, I have been fortunate to have had her help me with my own pets, and deeply value her support and guidance.

— JUDY KANE, ALIGNED CONSCIOUSNESS AND
AUTHOR OF *YOUR4TRUTHS: HOW BELIEFS IMPACT
YOUR LIFE*

In *Peace in Passing*, Maribeth shows us how very connected we are with our animals and how our thoughts and actions directly affect them and their well-being. She shares different perspectives from the animals she's communicated with so we can better understand what they are feeling. She presents specific techniques to help us navigate through the difficult process of aging and the eventual death of our beloved family pets. She also provides comprehensive information about alternative therapies that might help our animals enjoy a longer and better quality of life. Maribeth shares some comforting concepts on how our animals tell us things both before and after they have transitioned. *Peace in Passing* is filled with touching stories of animals and their human families as they support each other on the journey through the end of life. Having recently had my own dog transition, I've found *Peace in Passing* to be both enlightening and healing. I would highly recommend it to anyone who finds themselves caring for an aging pet.

— BONNIE KAYSER, SHENANDOAH SHEPHERD RESCUE

Peace in Passing is the book I wish I had had when my beloved Chelsea was alive! As I read the stories, I was immediately transported to the pivotal moments with Chelsea in her later years and as she transitioned. It truly gave me a sense of peace as I saw our journey in the journey of others in the book. Maribeth takes the reader along the journey of her communications with a variety of animals. The personality of each animal shines through her words. At the end, you understand just how much animals love unconditionally! Thank you, Maribeth, for showing us the beautiful world of animal communication.

— NICOLE MELTZER, INTUITIVE AUTHOR, SPEAKER,
AND TEACHER AT BALANCED U ACADEMY AND
AUTHOR OF THE UPCOMING BOOK,
INTUITIVE LANGUAGES

Maribeth's stories convey the message so well that, yes! you can communicate with your animals when they are with you and after they have passed.

— CONNIE JO MILLER, ALMOST LIFETIME SKEPTIC

When I lost my dog Buddy, Maribeth Decker's book, *Peace in Passing*, helped me understand the transition. I have taken great comfort in understanding that my beloved boy is still with me. I learned techniques I could use to connect with not only the dogs I had lost over the years, but also my current fur babies. In the edition, Maribeth provides additional guidance on connecting with your pet and using alternative healing methods like acupuncture and essential oils. You do not have to be "spiritual" to receive the comfort from the heartwarming stories shared throughout. Over the years, I have gifted this book to several of my friends who had pets that have transitioned to the other side.

— HEATHER C. MORROW

Peace in Passing is a great look into the energetic and spiritual world of our pets. Maribeth's skill and experience show us how we, as caregivers and pet guardians, can understand our pets and their experiences and delve into the relationship with our animals at a different level. The information in this book will help any pet guardian who has, or will, experience the loss of a beloved pet begins to understand and be reassured of the process. Maribeth's intuitive skills are such that she can help us know how our pets are feeling and how to better meet their needs.

Her stories of communication with animals and their progression through physical life changes and spiritual transformations is a solid reference of examples that we can use to gage our own interactions with our pets. With this kind of knowledge, we can have a more fulfilling and deeper connection with our pets and the animals around us.

— SCOTT MUZINSKI, DOCTOR OF CHIROPRACTIC DC,
NATUROPATHIC MEDICAL DOCTOR NMD, AND
ACUPUNCTURE PRACTITIONER, INTEGRATIVE
CHIROPRACTIC AND NATURAL MEDICINE

Peace in Passing by Maribeth Decker is at least a five-star book: it's easy to read, includes interesting true stories, a smooth flow of ideas, and tons of helpful information. I wish I had read it many, many years ago! It would have made a big difference in how I handled the deaths of my pets throughout a very long lifetime, and also in how I related to them during their lives.

Good ideas abounded in the book! Some of the ones I really liked are grief support groups through shelters, hospice care, honoring the animal's need for peace and comfort, having a memorial service, convening a welcoming party on the other side of the Rainbow Bridge, and creating a permanent memorial.

— MARYNANCE SCHELLENBACH, RETIRED LITURGIST, POET, AND ARTIST

Peace in Passing is a heartfelt guide to dealing with transitions of our beloved animals. It is loaded with nuggets of practical and profound wisdom. The true and heartwarming stories throughout the book open the mind and the heart to the deep connections that exist between animals and their people. I love Maribeth Decker's detailed guidance on how we can communicate with our animals, past and present. She manages to take a topic that is so difficult for most of us and turn it into an uplifting, inspiring experience. She also guides us through the many different healing modalities, alternative therapies, and much more. Her book is brilliantly written with love, compassion, and humor.

— MICHELE SILVA-DOCKERY, MATH EDUCATOR, REIKI MASTER

My appreciation for *Peace in Passing* comes from Maribeth's comforting guidance through the later stages of a pet's journey. In our culture, we're geared to prevent death and are unprepared to walk with an animal through to their transition. Through education and shared experiences, Maribeth encourages participation in these heartfelt times—to be with and learn from—these patient teachers, embrace the whole journey, and experience unfathomable love.

— TERRI SYMONDS GROW, FELINE HEALTH EXPERT,
ADVOCATE, AND EDUCATOR

PEACE IN PASSING

PEACE IN PASSING

COMFORT FOR LOVING HUMANS
DURING ANIMAL TRANSITIONS SECOND EDITION

MARIBETH COYE DECKER, MS, MGA

Edited by
DEBORAH KEVIN

HIGHLANDER
PRESS

To my dogs Timmie, Eddy, Mitsubishi and Tibor, who started me on this path.

How lucky I am to have [someone who] makes saying goodbye so hard.

- Winnie The Pooh

CONTENTS

FOREWORD

TINA ZION

When Maribeth Decker asked me to write the forward for *Peace in Passing*, I was first surprised, then honored, and then my heart was touched. As I began to read the rich, sincere, and profound knowledge in this book, a very old moment rose up in my memory.

One day, I sat, somewhat patiently, in the car line of my grandchildren's elementary school. I saw my first granddaughter step out through the school doorway with a smile on her face. A few moments later the older granddaughter came through the door and walked toward my car. She was still not smiling. There was a strange sadness on her nine-year-old face. She managed to hold back the tears until she sat in the back seat of the car and closed the door. I looked into the rearview mirror and saw silent tears flowing over her red cheeks.

I pulled the car over into a parking space and turned in my seat to look directly at her.

My sweet girl erupted into gasping sobs. "My teacher told us today, that animals do not have souls! Grandma, is that true?"

I said, "That is not true at all. Think about the times when you look into Skeeter's eyes. Picture that right now in your mind...you are looking into your dog's soul. Your teacher just does not know what you and I know. He has not had any education about animals or how smart they are, and no one has taught him about their souls."

Maribeth Decker's book, *Peace in Passing*, is brilliant and is the ultimate guidebook about animals and the relationships with their humans. She explains the steps to intuitively communicate with our animal loved ones. She directs the reader to feel and know the natural interconnectedness and how to trust the intuitive knowledge that the animals send to us.

This book shows us how to live together and how to directly assist in our animal's health. She offers detailed healing methods that you might not have known or even heard before. This book also actively guides us through our animal's natural physical decline. We also learn that communication is quite possible and quite healing after their transition into the non-physical realm.

Ms. Decker offers the most beautiful true-life stories that animals and their humans have shared with her. She details the communication that she receives as they become ill and begin their transition. She clearly interacts with them after crossing over into the spirit realm and helps you understand that you have that ability to communicate as well.

Ms. Decker's loving, gentle book of wisdom shines light into the depths that we humans feel for the animals that share their lives with us. She leads us though our own human transformation as we participate in the transformation between life and death of our cherished animals.

Even you animal lovers...yes, even you, will hold this book as the ultimate guide for your animal's health and then their transition into spirit realms.

May this book bless your life and the lives of your beloved animals.

Tina Zion
Fourth generation intuitive medium, acclaimed author of two First Place Gold Book Awards, and expert teacher of intuition and medical intuition around the globe.

INTRODUCTION

❝ Curiously enough, the unexplained perceptiveness of animals has been ignored not only by mainstream scientists but also by most psychic researcher and parapsychologists.Why?[P]sychic phenomena were seen as peculiarly human rather than as part of our biological heritage.

— RUPERT SHELDRAKE, AUTHOR OF *DOGS THAT KNOW WHEN THEIR OWNERS ARE COMING HOME*

In the last five years, I've had so many profound experiences helping people and their animals through the transition process that I decided to write an expanded version of my *Peace in Passing* book.

I feel compelled to start this edition by giving you permission to discover how you connect with your animal—whether they've passed on or they're still "on the planet."

By reading this book, you've already accepted my challenge: It's time for you to find your own intuitive strengths and abilities. What I share here is an open door, an invitation, a "what if," for you to find your own way into the sacred mystery of our relationship with animals. And life.

We all have our own wisdom, knowing about what works for us and our animals. I invite you to use this book's guidance as a torch to light up your own path. Find information that lights you up, that celebrates your own unique way of connecting. Don't get stuck in dogma —find the truth of existence in your relationship with your animals and the Divine.

I originally wrote this book because it became clear that, for many animal lovers, losing your animal companion can be as hard or harder than losing your family and friends. This is because, in addition to losing a loved one, most of the time *we* must decide when and how to let our animals go. It is a terrible burden.

Many of us feel guilty about our decisions, wondering if we did the right thing. Did we release them too early? Did we wait too long? Did they suffer?

After they are gone, we miss them fiercely. Because others often don't acknowledge the depths of our grief ("It was only an animal, for goodness sake, get over it!"), we don't feel safe sharing our grief like we do when a human relative or friend dies. But we go through the same grieving process as people do when beloved friends and family die. We want to find a way to feel peace about the loss in a way that honors our feelings of grief and our mutual love with our animal.

This book is designed to show you the way to not only grieve, but to honor your animal and your relationship long after they have passed on.

I will use real-life stories to help you find peace and experience a connection with the animal you have lost. In this expanded version, we will explore:

- Alternatives to not knowing when and how to let your animal go, and how to resolve feelings of guilt about your decision
- A framework—a way of viewing the transition process—to

help you and your animals before, during, and after the transition process.

- Ways to plan the transition so it reflects the love you feel for your animals
- An expansion of our understanding of the spiritual nature of our relationship with animals. This can allow you to view your loss differently so you may process and move more smoothly through the despair and grief that ensues after death. Feel free to incorporate whatever resonates into your own spiritual beliefs.
- Ways to incorporate animal communication techniques into your current communication with your animal. I've noticed that people who work with me already have an intuitive connection with their animals. Since you've been drawn to this book, let's believe you also have an intuitive connection with your animals. Incorporating these techniques will help you KNOW that whatever you receive from your animal is real, which brings so much comfort.
- The importance of re-examining our relationship with non-humans on the planet to bolster decisions that support sustainability for all living beings.

I feel and remember all the animals in my life who have moved on. I have felt people's pain, including my own, before, during, and after the loss of an animal. I have been transformed by my work with our animal friends as they lived and after they transitioned. I also know the great joy my animals have given me from listening to them and learning from them. I have witnessed the release of guilt and the cloaking of comfort that enfolded my clients as they learned to accept the spiritual nature of our animal companions.

I want to thank all the people (and their animals) who allowed me to share their stories. Their stories are the "stars" of my book. They brought this book to life!

After reading this book, you will:

- Know in your heart and mind that you have or will make a good decision about the timing of your animal's transition
- Be able to thoughtfully create your animal companion's exit strategy that reflects your love for your non-human family member
- Feel a connection to your animal beyond death
- Feel your animal's love every time you remember them
- (Maybe) begin to view all animals, even those we don't live with, as valued companions on our earthly journey.

1

THE RIGHT MINDSET FOR PEACE

> For most of us, ... more is needed. And that more is a leap of faith, an assurance that that which has been created with love is not going to be abandoned. Love does not create and then annihilate.
>
> — MADELEINE L'ENGLE, FORWARD TO *A GRIEF OBSERVED* BY
> C.S. LEWIS[1]

I HAVE a strong background in the basic sciences—I took pre-med courses while I was getting a bachelor's degree in psychology. Okay, organic chemistry about killed me, but I liked math. I liked figuring things out logically and methodically. I spent a lot of my time in my last job writing policies and procedures.

But regular science and logic aren't enough. I'm not saying you have to discount what we have learned from regular science. I certainly do not. However, a strictly logical, rational Newtonian mindset about how the world works will not allow you to experience a deep connection with your animal companion.

You must also accept the spiritual side of your relationship. Your animals are your family, and just as you have a spiritual (think heart) connection with your parents, siblings, and children, you connect spiritually with your animals. It's there whether or not you know it or accept it. Knowing and accepting, though, will make your connections stronger and more rewarding.

BRIEF PRIMER ON QUANTUM PHYSICS

Quantum physics, the study of how subatomic particles function, may provide a scientific basis for what we now know through intuition and experience. It is *incredibly* different than the Classical (Newtonian) physics I learned in college, which explained how the physical world worked.

Look up quantum physics theories if you're interested. If you're like me, start with something that has the equivalent of "For Dummies" at the end of the title. Regardless, here are some examples of how science is exploring the other side:

- Albert Einstein wrote, "Energy cannot be created or destroyed; it can only be changed from one form to another."
- Everything exits as both energy (waves) and solids (particles).[2]
- Subatomic particles seem to exist outside of the dimensions of time and space until they are observed.
- Subatomic particles are affected by intentions and thoughts. Scientific experiments at Princeton University found that scientists' intentions influenced the outcome of a random event generator (REG).[3]

What I make of this is as follows:

- If the personality and essence of a living being is energetic, then it may change form but not cease to exist. If thoughts, intentions and feelings are real and have physicality, which are expressed as waves (even if they are not solid), they have the capacity to affect us the same as a punch in the jaw or a warm hug. If reality is only reality when someone is observing it, the possibilities for what's real explode!

- Classical physics explains the universe and everything in it as elaborate machines, but intent and belief cannot influence machines, right? It doesn't make sense from a Newtonian physics perspective. However, experiments are showing that intentions do affect outcomes of non-aware subatomic particles. There's more going on from quantum physics.
- If you remain in the mindset of classical physics, you will miss out on the good stuff that will bring you peace.

I challenge you to discover for yourself how quantum physics theories give nightmares to logical, rational Classical physics mindsets! And it leaves us wondering what reality is. That's a great place to start opening up to the possibility of connecting intuitively to our animals while they live and after they have passed and seeing the wonders of their lives.

MYTHS ABOUT ANIMALS AND ANIMAL TRANSITIONS

66 Besides love and sympathy, animals exhibit other qualities connected with the social instincts which in us
would be called moral.

— CHARLES DARWIN

LET'S explore a few myths that keep us stuck in grief over the death
of our animals. Some of these myths are or were widely held scientific
beliefs which are being replaced by new scientific knowledge. Some
seem to be New Age beliefs that are human-centric and don't allow
animals to be individuals with their own purpose in incarnating and
living on this planet.

I commend your desire to make sense of your animal's life and
death. I am glad you are willing to re-think the many beliefs we have
held about animals in our lives.

Everyone has their own way of discovering the purpose of their
life. In addition to religious and spiritual traditions, animal lovers like
us have another dimension to explore if we choose.

You have already started to open this non-physical dimension
through your relationship with your animals at the end of their lives.

It will provide you with a level of connection to your animals and Spirit that is both heartwarming and heart-expanding. It will open you up in a new, deeper way to the goodness and richness of life.

MYTH: ANIMALS ARE BIOLOGICAL MACHINES

Some models of animal behavior contend animals are just biological machines driven by instinct and genes. You feed them and they become conditioned to come to you for food. All their behaviors are driven by survival and genetics.

There have been scientific theories that believed animals had no feelings. They did not even feel pain. I attribute this belief—and the belief that animals' lives are trivial—to peoples' continuing willingness to experiment on them and treat them in ways we would never allow with our own animals.

More recent scientific studies have demonstrated many animals' need for companionship and family ties, and their desire to raise their young. The lovely videos showing affection and friendship between different species, sometimes between predator and prey, show they are not biological machines.

To bring this discussion back to transitions, your animals will have wants and desires as they decline. This is in addition to the data you receive on their physical condition. You have a right and responsibility to decide what medical interventions will be done for and on your animals. You still have the right to listen to your heart —not to just what you want, but what your animal desires, in addition to how to keep them comfortable and enjoying some aspects of life.

I've worked with some animals that wanted to stick around a couple more months and their person held off. Other animals wanted to stick around, but their bodies were no longer able to sustain life any longer. We shared, "Adeline, you're going to get very uncomfortable soon. So, we're going to let you go before that happens because we love you."

I've also heard animals say, "I'm done, I'm tired, let me go, please."

Others were okay with sticking around a bit longer so their human could get emotionally ready for the transition.

It's a judgement call, but it's yours to make. You are receiving information about your animal; just open up. It may come in a flash, picture, or thought. I have worked with dreams for more than thirty years, so sometimes information comes to me when I wake up. Listen to the information because you know this soul better than anyone else.

MYTH: DEATH ENDS YOUR RELATIONSHIP

Many of us have heard stories from relatives or have had personal experiences of our *human* family members visiting after they died. If you haven't heard any good stories like this, ask older relatives. You might be surprised. You'll find they have been contacted by human family members who passed. They'll probably be delighted to share their stories with you.

My first husband, Winston, came to me in dreams for a period after he died in 1998. And my Gramie told me that a few days after Grampa died, she woke up from a nap and saw him standing in front of her. He had had a brain aneurysm and died while he was out with friends.

She blurted out, "What are you doing here? You're dead!" Grampa vanished. She wished she had said something more like, "Oh, boy, I miss you; so glad you are here!" Still, she was comforted because his last words were, "I'll see you later," and he kept his promise.

Animals' Energy Dissipates and Goes Back to Creator/Source When They Die

I discovered there's a belief in some circles that animals don't survive as separate personalities in the afterlife. Instead, their life force dissipates as a little cloud of energy and is inhaled back into Source without a second thought. They are gone forever. To console us, we're told we'll always have their memories in our hearts. So, it's really okay. All we need to do is get into a Yoga pose and breathe deeply.

Hogwash!

First off, how do we humans get off deciding that our personalities get to survive death, but animals—who were created by the same Being as humans—don't meet the "life after death" standard. Just because they're not human?

Those of us who have known our animals fully know they have memories, thoughts, feelings, wants, likes, and dislikes, just like humans. Maybe we don't understand them, but we know there is an internal life in them, just as there is in us.

Are we that in love with ourselves that no other species deserve an afterlife? Come on. Speciesism (the assumption of human superiority over other life forms) exists even in "enlightened" circles, it seems.

If you believe in an afterlife, and believe the Creator loves all his/her creatures, why wouldn't animals survive death?

And, if you dream about your version of heaven, isn't the dream so much happier if your animals are with you? Why would we be denied a reunion with our animals as well as with our human loved ones?

Death is Not the End

The relationship between you and your animal companion has changed with their death. You can't touch your animal. But, they still care for you, and you certainly still care for them. You can still talk to them, and they can still listen. They have another life in another place, but you are still at the top of their "greatest hits" list. They are checking on you and even watching over you.

In many cases, they make their presence known to those they love after they have passed. I have connected with animals many times after they have passed. I have seen animals who have passed, felt their presence, and carried on intelligent conversations with them. They can have extraordinary insights into their guardians' current lives and challenges.

Our transitioned animals keep an eye on those they love, just as our beloved relatives do. They are still interested in how we're doing. I don't think they obsess over us, but they do check in on us, and they will come when we ask them to. We can still talk to them and know we are heard.

My personal experience has shown that animals do, in fact, survive death. I didn't do a scientific research project, but neither did the folks who decided animal energy goes poof after they die!

I've seen my dog Timmie as a full-body apparition while I was making dinner. It was as if he was physically present. Not the see-though ghostly type apparition in all the good ghost stories I read through my life. No, he was so real I was sure I could pet him.

I checked my "Am I crazy?" meter. Anyone who knows me will tell you the answer is no. Odd, but not crazy. I was clean and sober, and there he was, letting me know he was happy. He wanted me to know that.

Timmie. Photo credit: Maribeth Decker

I've also collected many stories from people who've had a wonderful experience of their animal making themselves known. You'll find some good ones later in the book.

Do your own research. Ask people if they thought their animals stopped by after death. They'll say, "I probably made this up, but I swear, I heard—I saw—I dreamed—I felt." And, then they'll tell you a story that's so heartwarming, you'll know their animals came through for them.

Just one experience opens us to the possibility. Two experiences make us a believer.

Believe.

MYTH: THE DEATH OF AN ANIMAL COMPANION IS A TRIVIAL EXPERIENCE

Not by a long shot is the death of your animal a trivial experience. Most of our animals provide emotional sustenance and physical companionship, remind us how to play and smile, and see the good in our lives. They allow us to touch and caress another live being, to feel that warmth and positive response to our touch. More than that, they ask for our loving touch. They communicate they like and love us. They do it every day. They remind us there is more to life than work.

We also carry the burden of having to choose the time and place for ending their life. We struggle with the inability to know if they're ready to go and how to explain why we are letting them go. These factors create a difficult emotional experience we do not recover from easily.

When a beloved human family member is terminally ill, colleagues expect we will take time off to care for their needs and be there as necessary. When that person dies, there is a funeral. We are expected to take time off from work, and people may even bring dinner and help with chores. People ask how we are. They understand and accept the tears or choked voice when we express our grief. They are patient with the recovery process.

Contrast this with animal transitions. We have to minimize our grief and pretend we are handling it. There is no funeral; we are expected to move on quickly. So, on top of the grief and the anxiety over making the decision to end a life, we don't get to grieve fully and do not get much support in recovering from the grieving process.

I am here to say: It's hard, and it's not a trivial experience. You have my permission to grieve, to find someone to talk to about how unique and brilliant your animal was, and what crazy things your animal did. You can think about them, cry, and miss them.

But, please don't stay there. Read on.

MYTH: YOU MUST HAVE A SPECIAL GIFT TO COMMUNICATE WITH YOUR ANIMAL

If you believe this myth, you're cutting yourself off from experiencing real moments of contact with your animal. The fact that so many people from all walks of life communicate with their animals during their transition period debunks this myth. I am inundated with stories of what people have felt, seen, and heard through this time.

Our bodies are wired to receive information from sources beyond the five senses. Thoughts, physical feelings, memories, and emotions are vibrations that can be discerned by our minds if we open up to those vibrations.

Our heart connection to our animals is refreshingly real. Animal communication in its finest form is a heart-to-heart connection. And, it's strong. It's available to all those who open their minds as well as their hearts. Believe that it's possible. Set your intention to make decisions for *their* wellbeing. Sadly, this will include a time when staying in their body is not for their highest good anymore.

Have you ever heard yourself saying, "If Timmie could talk, I'd swear he just said..." Well, you just had an intuitive connection and communication with your animal! It's not rocket science. It's quantum physics science with a big batch of love energizing the communication.

The Science Behind the Intuitive Connection with Our Animals

Lucky for us, quantum physics provides a way to explain telepathic connections. Classical laws of physics are great for explaining how the world works on a molecular level (gravity is wonderful, right?), but it has nothing to say about beings connecting at a subatomic level.

I am not a quantum physicist, so my explanation is probably somewhere below "Quantum Physics for Dummies." Feel free to explore more on your own.

Everything is Energy

Let's start with Einstein's equation, $E = mc^2$. Energy = mass times a constant squared. That means everything in our world is energy. Even mass, which looks solid and impacts us on a physical level (sight, smell, touch, hearing), is also waves of energy. It's just vibrating slower when it's physical.

A good analogy is water. When it vibrates very slowly, it's ice. When it vibrates faster, it's water. If it continues to vibrate faster, it becomes steam and then water vapor. We don't see water vapor in the atmosphere, but it still exists.

Emotions are energy, thoughts are energy. Memories are energy. In our 3D world, they cannot be seen like we see a dog or a house. But, they have a physicality on the quantum level.

So, when someone (including our animals) experiences an emotion, thinks a thought, has a memory, or feels pain, they have created an energetic vibration.

Energy Cannot Be Created or Destroyed

Einstein also says energy can neither be created or destroyed. So, if something physical existed, the only thing it can do is change form—not disappear forever. This explains why I can connect with animals who have passed; their energy lives on in a different form.

A Second Reality

Quantum physics experiments have shown that at the subatomic level, stuff acts very differently from what we experience. The "laws" of time, space, and distance do not apply. So while we operate in the world of cause and effect, and experience time as linear, there is another reality superimposed on existence. This other reality is what's going on at the subatomic level. Becoming aware of it is the key to understanding why we can receive and send information intuitively.

Experiments have shown that:

- The universe is connected outside of time and space. Some liken it to a spider web. A vibration at any part of the web can be felt on any part of the web.
- Consciousness influences objects we would consider inanimate, like subatomic particles.

How Our Body Receives Information

Our brain is designed to take energy and translate it into information.

Technically, our eyes do not see, our ears do not hear, our skin does not feel, our taste buds do not taste, and our nose does not smell. They collect data/energy and send it to the brain. The brain translates it into sight, sound, feeling, taste, and smell.

When you get this, *really get this*, possibilities open up. If we use the correct vibration of energy, we could, through our intentions, transmit thoughts, feelings, sounds, memories, or smells to another on a subatomic level. We could receive them as well. Our brain could translate them into information using our senses.

Different Senses; Different Information

When I started developing my intuition, I felt my abilities were very limited. I compared myself to others, who were receiving incredible visuals. I'm sharing this so that you can relax, be okay with wherever you're starting, and not get discouraged. Feel good about yourself because you're probably way ahead of where I started!

Develop Your Intuition

The key to developing your intuition is to start paying attention to what you are receiving.

Intuition comes before regular thought. Intuition comes before regular thought. I'll say it again: INTUITION COMES BEFORE REGULAR THOUGHT.

As medical intuitive Tina Zion says, "Look for that quick POP of information. Notice it, don't let it go. Intuition is constant and consistent."[4]

Regular thought bounces all over the place. You may get thoughts or questions or rationalizations about how it's true or not.

Bottom line: Don't dismiss the first thing you receive. Welcome it! Write it down or even draw a picture if that helps you remember. I do.

~

Butch: You Will Know It's Time

I worked with Laura to see if her dog Butch was ready to transition. He had serious physical issues, lots of achiness, and definitely slowing down. Butch told me, "My body's old. I'm okay with the aches and pains right now. But I'll let Laura know when I've had it." We asked how Butch would let Laura know. He said with certainty, "I'll give Laura a look. She'll know."

Laura contacted me to let me know that, indeed Butch had kept his word. She woke up one morning and immediately went to check on Butch. Butch slowly raised his head to stare at her with love. Full of intention to connect, Laura knew without a doubt that Butch was giving her the look as promised. She released him from his body shortly afterward. Although she was full of grief, she knew Butch was ready.

~

MYTH: OUR ANIMAL COMPANIONS DO NOT HAVE RICH, INNER LIVES

One of the positive results of the Internet is the sharing of videos showing behaviors we thought only humans were capable of—grieving, funeral rites, problem solving, using tools, compassion towards prey animals, and unlikely friendships between species.

~

Gustav: A Stuffed Hedgehog[5]

Liz Guthridge of Connect Consulting Group, shared about her dog, Gustav, in her November 17, 2015, blog titled, "3 good behavior lessons from Gustav"[6]:

> Gustav's most amazing gesture was toward one of my clients who had given him a stuffed hedgehog. Once Gustav unwrapped the toy, he ignored it. (He preferred stuffed birds.)
>
> Many months later, this client came to our house for a walk we were going to take together with Gustav. He welcomed her and then retreated. He returned with the hedgehog, which he brought to her. She was elated.
>
> I was dumbfounded. How did Gustav even remember he had that toy, much less who had given it to him? But I didn't want to reduce my client's joy, so I kept my mouth shut. Was it her scent on the toy? Something else? And how did he know how much she'd appreciate his gesture? I'll never know. However, his actions that day continue to resonate with me, and I try very hard to honor him by being kind and empathetic.

(By the way, Gustav 'told' me he'd stand next to the cardboard Pope in return for a stuffed toy rooster he spotted in a bin near the Pope.)

Photo credit: Liz Guthridge

Goldie: Eavesdropper

When Dr. Scott Muzinski told me how his cat listened in to his family's conversation, I grinned from ear to ear. I've worked with Dr. Scott and his wife Dr. Kim for a few years now. They have three animals I've had the pleasure of working with. There's a wonderful dog, Thomas, who reminds me of my dog, Tibor, and they have two great cats, Goldie and Tookie. Here's what Scott shared about his cat Goldie listening in:

Photo credit: Dr. Scott Muzinski

Interestingly, today Kim and Sam (my son) were sitting in the TV room while I was doing chores. They talked about how well we take care of our pets as they worked on our cat Goldie, balancing her hip and other things. (Maribeth's note: They are an energy-healing, holistic chiropractic family.)

Then, Kim and Sam had a discussion. "I hope [our animals] appreciate the things we get for them. Like the cat stairs to the couch! Oh, and that new water fountain with flowing water. And don't forget the bed that looks like a footstool (nicknamed the chicken coop) for them to sleep in!"

At that instant, our cat Goldie got up, walked over to the stairs, and walked down them. Then she walked over to the water fountain and took a big drink. Finally, she walked to the 'chicken coop' (the bed), went inside, and laid down. She looked right back out at us.

"I'm grateful, okay? Are you happy?" she seemed to be saying to Kim and Sam.

~

Mystery Dog: An Irish Tale

Jen Kline Clark of The Profit Vortex and her husband, once visited Ireland and spent a Sunday morning driving around the Irish countryside, loving every minute. That is, until their car broke down. Moving over to the side of the road, they wondered what they should do. They tried the usual restarting of the engine to no avail. They decided to flag down the next passing car.

But it was an early Sunday morning. They settled down for a long wait since people were probably in church. A dog came over the hill and stopped. He stared and stared at them, and then turned back around the way he came. *Well, that was odd,* they thought.

A while later, the dog came back with two men from the local pub. The men told them the dog was acting strangely and wanted the men to follow him. They left the pub reluctantly, until they saw the broken-down car.

Coming over to Jen and her husband, they saw their trouble. They soon figured out the problem, brought a truck with tools over, and got the car started again!

Profusely thanking the men *and* the dog, Jen and her husband continued on their tour of the Irish countryside.[7]

~

Although these stories aren't about transition, they are delightful tales of animals' thought processes.

MYTH: ANIMALS MUST BE TAKEN TO THE VETERINARIAN TO BE EUTHANIZED

When I was younger, smaller animals—those that lived in the house—had to be taken to the veterinarian for euthanasia. That was the way it was: Death in a veterinarian office.

When I took my dog Missy in to be euthanized, tears streamed down my face. I waited in the reception area for a room, holding Missy close. We finally went into an exam room, not designed for comfort, but for efficiency and cleanliness. I remember how hard it was to walk out after the procedure and the difficulty of finalizing paperwork in the reception area. Tears gushed as I walked out to my car without my beloved Missy. The difficult loss was made worse as it felt so public.

When I'm waiting in the lobby of a veterinarian's office, I know when someone just let their animals go. Heartbroken humans are easy to spot in a veterinarian's office. Their grief touched all of us, because we know what waits for us.

People who have horses have always known there was another way. When they are ready to release their horse, the veterinarian comes to the horse.

If you take your animal to the veterinarian to be euthanized, maybe bring a soft blanket for them. Be there with your animal if you can. It will comfort you both.

If you can, consider having a veterinarian come to your home, as this comforts us and our animals. Who would want to die at a place known for vaccinations and hard tables?

At home, your extended family can be with them and say goodbye if they choose. Even if it's just to drop by and give a final hug, it's wonderful.

~

Mitsubishi: Passing at Home

We knew Mitsubishi wasn't interested in any more medical interventions at the end of his life. We brought him to a very good veterinary hospital, and even after treatment, he had lost the use of his back legs and was incontinent. We talked to our vets and found a service that would euthanize him in our home and take his body away afterwards.

That day, we carried him into the living room and put him on a waterproof pad. Our neighbors came over to spend time with him and brought their dogs to say goodbye. Kids in the neighborhood stopped by to say goodbye to Mitsu and to give him treats. My son came over and my daughter came up from college to be with him. Our little dog, Stella, stayed around because she knew something was up. Mitsubishi basked in the attention and the treats. He was in no pain. When the vets came, it was an easy transition.

That night, an acquaintance, who did not know Mitsubishi had passed, called me. At this time, I was not consciously connecting with animals. I told her I had to release Mitsu from his body. She called because she had the feeling something had happened. Then she told me she could connect with animals and explained that Mitsu was doing just fine. I was grateful and surprised at the same time!

∿

MYTH: ANIMALS ALWAYS UNDERSTAND THEIR FAMILY MEMBER WHO PASSED ISN'T COMING BACK

I used to think animals in the family always understood what happened when their human or another animal in the family passed on. This isn't necessarily true. I have met animals who feel confused and sad when their human or animal companion is no longer with them. They wonder what has happened to the other animal and/or their guardians when they die.

When you need to take your animal to the veterinarian's office for euthanasia, your other animals may assume it's just a regular visit to the vet. They can be quite concerned when only you return home. You'll notice they'll keep looking for their person or their animal friend.

They may still be confused even when the euthanasia happens at home. Be sure to allow them to take a sniff of your animal after they've transitioned. It may help them realize their friend has passed on.

Still, some do understand when one of their family is getting ready to transition. I enjoyed reading about a cat named Oscar who sat with people in the Steere House Nursing and Rehabilitation Center just before they passed. It happened often enough that Dr. David Dosa wrote a book about Oscar.[8] While Oscar's story is wonderful, it's important to realize that some animals do not understand what's happening.

You can help your animals navigate through this. Communicate with the animals left behind that their family member isn't returning physically. Picture the deceased person or animal as healthy and happy when you talk to your animals. Act as if those left behind understand.

If the person or animal had been sick, remind your animals that they probably sensed (smelled) the illness and maybe the discomfort in their friend. They probably knew their family member was declining and not getting better.

There is much evidence that demonstrates dogs can sense various illnesses in humans.[9] Why wouldn't they sense illness in another animal?

Bestselling author Maria Goodavage wrote an excellent book, *Doctor Dogs: How Our Best Friends Are Becoming Our Best Medicine*.[10] She writes about dogs sensing illness in patients all over the world.

Cats have an even better sense of smell than dogs, so I'm sure they knew something was changing in their friend. As far as my research goes, I found that mammals we hang out with (horses, rabbits, guinea pigs, rats) have a better sense of smell than humans. And the most recent research has *overturned* the incorrect belief that birds don't have a strong ability to smell.[11] So, assume your animal knew their friend was declining.

I've met a few healthy animals who worried that they were going to be the next to disappear from the house, just like their dog or cat friend. They weren't thinking so much about dying, but that they'd be rehomed or sent back to the shelter. If you have an animal that went through a few residences before they landed in your forever home, let them know they're not going anywhere. Their animal friend's body just couldn't continue. Tell them their friend is safe and loved!

MYTH: ANIMALS LEFT BEHIND DO NOT GRIEVE

Some people have written about how animals are always "in the know." There is no looking back or looking forward.

Even certain scientists have proposed theories that animals do not have memories or emotions. They are simply organic machines that react to whatever stimulus comes along.

This seems shortsighted. I wonder if these people have ever had a deep, fulfilling relationship with an animal—if they've ever gotten beyond their human-centric view to fully "see" this beautiful being and notice this being's experience.

When a companion has been a part of an animal's life for years, how could that animal not notice that that companion is gone? That the routines they experienced together, for better or for worse, are no longer part of their life? Of course, they notice! In some situations, it is clear to me animals really can miss their people or their animal family members.

Here are a few real-life stories of animals who grieved the loss of a loved one.

∿

Hachikō: Loyal Companion

When I was stationed with the U.S. Navy in Japan, I saw a statue of a dog at Shibuya railroad station in Tokyo. I learned it was in memory of a dog named Hachikō. Here's his story:

> In the 1920s, a professor at the University of Tokyo, Dr. Ueno, adopted an Akita and named him Hachikō. This loyal dog always waited near Shibuya Train station for Dr. Ueno to arrive home from work so they would walk home together. A year later, Professor Ueno died at work. Not understanding what happened to his beloved human, Hachikō came to Shibuya Station every day for almost ten years hoping to walk Professor Ueno home.

After Hachikō's story was published in the *Asahi Shimbun*, folks started giving Hachikō food and treats.

When Hachikō died, his ashes were buried next to his beloved Professor Ueno.

Hachikō. Photo credit: Max Khoo, Shutterstock

Now, every April 8, there's a special ceremony at Shibuya Station remembering Hachikō's devotion. Tons of dog people show up to honor his good-hearted loyalty.

The University faculty even commissioned a bronze statue of Professor Ueno coming back to greet Hachikō.[12]

I often see Hachikō's devotion in animals who are bewildered about where their human or their animal companion has gone. It is painful. I love it when I bring an animal who has passed and their buddy who is still alive together through animal communication. Lately, I've invited their person to join me in imagining them reunited in a Sacred Space of love and healing. As I see them greet each other, I show the animal who's still "on the planet" that the animal who has passed is doing great, bringing peace into everyone's lives.

~

Capitan: Cemetery Watchdog

Miguel Guzmán of Cordoba, Argentina, brought Capitan, a German Shepherd, home for his son Damien in 2015. Unfortunately, Mr. Guzmán died unexpectedly in 2016. Capitan ran away from home the next day. Mrs. Guzmán and Damien frantically searched for Capitan, finally finding him at the cemetery where Mr. Guzmán was buried. It was forty-five minutes away! Astoundingly, Capitan had never been taken to the cemetery.

The family tried to bring Capitan home, but he would escape and return to the cemetery. They finally let him stay at the cemetery, where the workers fed him.

The cemetery directors say Capitan walks around the cemetery during the day. But, at 6:00 p.m., Capitan returns to Miguel Guzmán's grave to sleep on it.[13]

~

Greyfriars Bobby: Loyalty for Life

This story has its unbelievers, but knowing about the story of Hachikō, I don't doubt it. Ben Johnson shares Bobby's story on the Historic UK site.[14] Here's the short version:

In 1850, John Gray arrived in Edinburgh, Scotland, and joined the Edinburgh Police Force as a night watchman. To keep him company through the long winter nights John took a partner, a small Skye Terrier, his watchdog, Bobby. John and Bobby became a familiar sight patrolling the streets of Edinburgh.

Greyfriars Bobby. Photo credit: Fabian Farber, Shutterstock

John died of tuberculosis on February15,1858, and was buried in Greyfriars Kirkyard. Bobby soon touched the hearts of the local residents when he refused to leave his master's grave, even in the worst weather conditions.

The keeper of Greyfriars tried on many occasions to evict Bobby from the Kirkyard. In the end he gave up and provided a shelter for Bobby by placing sacking beneath two table stones (large horizontal gravestones supported above ground) at the side of John Gray's grave. Bobby stayed by John's grave for fourteen years!

∽

Pixie: Wild Horses
I came across this story of a man who experienced wild horses saying goodbye to one of their own.

In his blog, *How Wild Horses Deal with Death and Grief: A Rare Insight*, William E. Simpson shared his poignant experiences of his friendship with a herd of wild horses on the Oregon-California border in the northwestern part of the United States.

Mr. Simpson found Pixie, a mare who he felt was a special friend, dying from an accident. She was surrounded by her herd and other herds. It's worth reading the whole story as long as you have tissues close by. Here's the horse-to-horse grieving that Mr. Simpson witnessed:

> And there, standing over her [Pixie] was a majestic guardian, a single bachelor stallion who Laura and I had named *Red Sox* a few years before. He was audibly crying over her lifeless body; making a haunting sound I have never heard a horse make before; a soul-piercing sound that I will never forget. It was like a whinny but with a hallowed, sad tone. This beautiful young stallion was one of Pixie's playmates as she grew up ... now he was the sentinel over her remains, lamenting her loss. I looked at him and asked and he moved back allowing me to go to Pixie's head to say my own goodbyes. When I was done and moved away, he moved back to where he had stood, directly over her.[15]

∼

Even if you're not sure that your animals have an affectionate relationship, trust that they are grieving on some level.

MYTH: IF WE'RE NOT WITH THEM WHEN THEY PASS, THEY DIED ALONE

And they judge us for how we handled their passing.

As I have asked animals this question from their worried human, I found that not to be true. Maybe it's because they are less entangled in the "what if" and "what could have been" than humans. Our animal friends spend more time in the here and now. They don't spend time figuring out whose fault it is.

Some animals understand when something is not right in their physical body. I worked with a dog who had cancer in his back right leg. His leg needed to be amputated. His person was worried that he was upset to lose the leg. What I received from him, though, told me the dog knew something was wrong with his leg. What came through was that his limb was like a rotten piece of meat.

It's so clear to me that the vibration of our love is what our animals take with them. So, if we made decisions from a place of love and compassion, that's what grounds them.

And when they are no longer in their body, their consciousness begins to expand, and they see things more clearly. They are not upset. They enjoy the freedom of an energetic body and lack of pain.

3

TRUTHS

> Birth in the physical [plane] is death in the spiritual
> [plane]. Death in the physical [plane] is birth in the
> spiritual [plane].
>
> — EDGAR CAYCE, *THE SLEEPING PROPHET*

SINCE WE DISCUSSED myths about animals and how they age, I wanted to share some truths I discovered while working with animals facing the end of their physical lives. The more you understand this time in your animal's life, the better you'll navigate it. I want to share more knowledge with you so you'll be open to new possibilities. Many of us feel stuck in our grief and worry about making bad decisions, which can limit how we can navigate this part of life.

So, take a deep breath, and open your mind and, more importantly, your heart. Look for how this information might help you and your animal make it through each day, each hour, each minute as they transition back to the spiritual plane of existence.

ANIMALS SENSE THAT THEIR BODIES ARE GIVING OUT

As animals age, most understand their body is giving out. Alternately, even if they're not clear what's next, they know what they're experiencing isn't fun. And, they are *tired*, physically and spiritually. They are ready to move on and don't seem to experience the fear humans have about death. Some worry about the humans they are leaving behind and stay longer than is comfortable for them, just to make sure their human is emotionally ready to let them go.

When we finally make the decision, we can let our animal companions know when the end will happen. If you get in tune with your animals, you can explain the details of the transition to them. You can tell them how it will happen and where it will happen. (Read Chapter 6, "Animal Communication Strategies" to find some ideas on communicating with your animal telepathically.)

When I'm communicating with an animal who's about to transition, I tell them that when the body dies, they should step up and out of it like they would step out of the house, car, or barn. I ask them to imagine they are on their way to their next life with ease and grace.

Be sure to set up a welcoming party from the other side to attend. All you have to do is ask. Invite their beloved family and friends, both human and animal, who have passed on to attend the transition to make sure it is a joyous occasion for the animal. Ask them to "show them the ropes." Doesn't the thought make you smile? This invitation can make the passing easier for everyone.

YOU'RE ALLOWED TO DISAGREE WITH YOUR VET

If your animal is in crisis, you will bring them to your veterinarian. Given your animal's condition, your veterinarian might recommend euthanasia right then and there.

This may take you by surprise, or you may have felt that your animal had passed the point of no return. Stop and give yourself permission to connect to your heart's assessment of the situation.

If you're not ready, acknowledge that to yourself. Consider your personal assessment of your animal's desire to stick around a bit longer. It's always your decision to release or not release your animal from their body. Give yourself permission to take them home if you're not quite ready.

Marynance was faced with this exact decision about her aging cat Samson, who was close to the end. When she took Samson to the veterinarian, the veterinarian was sure it was time to let him go. But Marynance had an intuitive connection to Samson like many of us do. And, she knew he wasn't ready. And she wasn't either. So, she decided to take him home. He enjoyed three more weeks of hanging out in the sun before she felt he was finally ready to move on. She had so much more peace because she listened to her heartfelt intuition about her animal. She told me, "I was really, really happy to have had that last brief time with him."

ANIMALS HAVE LAST REQUESTS

Your animal companions can share desires about letting go or staying on the planet with you longer. Some feel great in spite of their human receiving a diagnosis that they are terminal, so they have no reason to want to move on. Others feel pretty lousy but want to spend more time with their human before they pass. An animal may want to stick it out until her human returns home from a business trip, for instance. Some are ready to go when asked. They are in pain, life is not fun, and they are ready to move on. You know it, they know it, and they are okay with letting go.

They might also have requests about their passing. Your animal may have a desire about who is with them when they pass or a wish not to die alone. Furthermore, they might want to be outdoors or in a certain place they love.

Believe it or not, you can see if there's anything they'd like to do before they pass on. If you can honor it, it will be a lovely memory to counter the loss of your beloved animals.

~

Andrew: Life's a Party

In one of my sessions, Andrew, a dog with severe neurological issues, wasn't ready to leave this earth. I saw him in person and the extent of his issues was crystal clear. I asked him why he was sticking around. "I want my party," he told me. When I shared his wish with his people, I thought they would tell me I was nuts.

But, then the man looked at his girlfriend and said, "We always give Andrew a birthday party!"

The girlfriend excitedly explained to me, "Yes, we invite all his doggie cousins, bake a dog-friendly birthday cake, and they wear silly hats. He loves it!"

They knew exactly what to do for Andrew to help him move on.

~

Chazworth: Don't Let Me Die Alone

Chaz on a toboggan. Drawing by Maribeth Decker.

My longtime friend Debbie had a wonderful cat, Chazworth, who I had spent time with when visiting Debbie in my childhood hometown of Buffalo, New York. Chaz had a number of health issues, and Debbie asked me to check in with him to see if he was ready to pass. He showed me a couple of images, which I drew.

I'm sharing this one, because it was his way of saying, "I'm ready." I could see him standing on a toboggan going down a snowy hill with a scarf that stuck straight out, as if showing that he was going downhill fast. I also felt excitement from him. Put this together and you get, "I'm going downhill fast (health is failing) and I'm excited (about passing on)."

Debbie felt Chaz still had more time left, so she enjoyed her time with him while watching how he was faring physically. Sometime after this message, Chaz suffered another "slow down" and lost bladder control. We recontacted Chaz to see if he was ready to transition at this point. The answer was "yes."

But, he had a request—I still tear up when I share this—he said he did not want to die alone. This was an important piece of information because Debbie worked outside the house during the day. So, he was in the house alone during the work week.

Given his request, Debbie reluctantly made the appointment to let him go when she felt the time was right. Debbie did not let the veterinarian take him into another room to euthanize him. She stayed with Chaz as he transitioned, as he had requested. In her heart, Debbie knew Chaz was okay with her decision.

~

Glo: Yer a Wizard

Glo. Photo credit: Michelle F.

On our way home from a seminar, I shared with Michelle about how my friend's cat Chazworth had told me he did not want to die alone. Her family had told Michelle that her dog Glo had stopped eating and was having to be carried outside when she needed a bio break. Michelle received a message from Glo that she would like to be outside on the lawn. So, Michele called home and let them know Glo's wishes.

When she got home, Glo let her know she was ready to pass. Michelle thought about Chazworth's wishes and reasoned, well, who *would* want to die alone? So, she arranged to have Glo brought home. The family put Glo on the kids' Harry Potter blanket in the front yard and stayed with her during the transition. She was buried in the Harry Potter blanket, which delighted the kids.

Here's how I heard the story from Glo. "I was aware Michelle was more open, that a path of communication was available between us. She was thinking about me. My body was crap at that point. I gave her the picture of me being outside on the grass with the family around me. And she heard."

Glo showed me she was jumping with joy about how well the transition went.

Michelle reports she can feel Glo's presence and almost hear her delighted laughter when the kids are sharing stories about her.

ANIMALS WOULD LIKE TO SAY GOODBYE

Animals may want to share some last words for their beloved guardians about what they are grateful for and what they loved about sharing their lives together. Even when people know how much love there is between their animals and them, humans need reassurance that they're doing the right thing and that their animals agree with their decisions. Thankfully, animals are happy to share how much love they have for their humans. It's one of my favorite times in helping everyone get ready for the transition, because I usually receive a visual pulled from my childhood memories in the form of animated cartoons. For instance, sometimes I see a huge, pink heart beating in front of the animal's chest for their person. That conveys incredible, undying (yes, undying) love for their human.

At times, a beloved animal needs to hear that their human is ready to let them go. Often, the animal worries more about how their human will deal with their transition. They will ask if their person will be able to make it without them. You might want to be ready to tell your animal that you've prepared yourself and your family members. You promise you'll survive. You'll be very sad but relieved that they're not hurting anymore.

This opportunity to say goodbye and ask questions is not always available to our human friends and family. In many cases, though, we set the time and place of our animal's passing, giving us a chance to say goodbye, hear what they have to say, and tell them what we need to say to let them go. Nothing is left unsaid or worried about. It helps us let go of the totally understandable sense of guilt we feel for ending their physical life.

Take advantage of this truth. Use it to help you (and them) let go in a loving way. It is good, healthy, and peaceful for everyone.

ANIMALS HAVE A PURPOSE IN OUR LIVES

Our relationship with our animals is not random; they did not come into our lives by chance. We come together for a purpose. The most obvious purpose for most of us is companionship, and out of that, comes the expression of love.

Many times, animals provide a deep love for us without judgement, a quality that is hard to find in our human companions. How often do you find someone who is excited about seeing you *every single day* of their lives? Who always finds time to see how you're doing and give you a little love? To respond to your offer of love with appreciation and affection? Who thinks you are great company even if you're snoring? It's very good for our souls.

Aside from basic companionship, our animals can reflect issues in our lives back at us at times. Their behaviors, even the ones we don't love, may reflect something we need to look at in our life. When they are "bad," "acting out," or "misbehaving," we might want to stop and think what's up in our lives that might be triggering this.

For example, I went to our vet recently about some worrisome symptoms our dog Stella exhibited. Our vet wisely asked, "Is there anything going on in the house?" Animals are affected by our human challenges. Stella was reacting to the human drama around her. They also can absorb our negative emotions and release them for us to help us stay well and continue to function.

The most obvious example is when you are upset and begin petting your animal. Many times, the animal knows something is up, and your animal finds you and stays close. And you feel better![16] Studies have shown that people with animals live longer, and I think this is one of the reasons.[17,18] They relieve us of some of our anxiety, which keeps our bodies healthier.

ARE ANIMALS SIMPLY OUR MIRRORS?

I'd like to dive more deeply here. When we discuss our animals' issues, people sometimes declare, "It must be because of me because I've heard that animals are our mirrors!"

Animals as mirrors means animals' health issues and behaviors reflect what's going on with their humans. So, should we look to the humans in the family—and maybe blame them—for their animals' behavioral and physical issues? Not necessarily. As we just discussed, animals have a purpose in our lives, but this doesn't mean they simply exist as a mirror to reflect what's happening in our lives.

Believing animals are in our lives *solely to mirror our emotions and actions to help us grow* turns animals into reaction machines. We're the input, the stimulus, and they're the output, the reaction. It's another version of the early psychologists' and scientists' stimulus-response theories. B.F. Skinner comes to mind. (He believed free will was an illusion. Everything we do was in response to an outside stimulus.)

Making animals our mirrors is too strong a statement for me. Mirrors are two-dimensional, and our animals are not two-dimensional. This belief of animals as our mirrors takes away free will for our animals and focuses on us. It can't always be about us, can it?

Instead, I believe each animal has their own personality, peculiarities, and preferences. They are unique beings and have distinctive perceptions of what's happening in their life. Animals are autonomous. They have their own story and life path, which includes their humans. Lucky us!

To anchor this in for you, you've probably heard about an animal with a tough history. Many people believe the animal's pre-adoption life experiences shape their current less-than-wonderful behaviors.

My own experience is with my dog Tibor. In the beginning, he growled and bared his teeth when I tried to bring him into the house after a delightful walk. He wasn't mirroring my reluctance to return to the house. Instead, he was expressing his fear about going into the house. It got worse when I tried to pull him in. So, I stood inside and asked him to come in using loving words and feelings. It worked.

Tibor decided to come into the house. I honored his feelings, allowed him to express them (safely), and he willingly chose to come in.

I didn't create Tibor's door problem, but I could help him by listening with love to what he was trying to communicate and adjusting *my* behavior.

Sometimes we can see our animal's purpose more clearly after they have passed. Sometimes, too, our animals see their purpose more clearly after they have left their physical body; they seem to gain astounding clarity about their purpose in living with us. It is as if they have shed the limitations of being in a dog/cat/horse/bird. Their soul is more present to share insights with the human.

~

Eddy, Mitsubishi, and Tibor

My dog Eddy came into our life as I started dating Charlie, who became my second husband. Eddy took to Charlie, and it was clearly mutual. Charlie had not grown up with dogs, and the cats in the house were his mother's cats. I saw Eddy's role as providing Charlie with a real-life example of unconditional love. She was excellent at that!

Eddy and Patrick Coye. Photo credit: Maribeth Decker.

Mitsubishi was my companion after my first husband died. He jogged with me, went on road trips with us, and provided a mischievous joy of life that pulled me out of my grief before it became overwhelming.

Tibor, who is alive and well, was the key to my focus on animal communication. He continues to be the "canary in the mine" who detects when the vibrations in the house are not at their optimal level of love!

You might want to think about what your animals' purposes have been in your life.

~

WE HAVE A PURPOSE IN OUR ANIMAL'S LIVES

From the previous section, it's clear we can affect our animals' emotions and physical wellbeing, and influence their actions. The key is not to assume that's the only reason they're in our lives.

Having said all this, compassionate human beings bring love and acceptance, teach animals how to enjoy life, and how get along with others. For many of our adopted animals, we show them that not all humans are bad; some of us are quite lovely and loving. They are allowed to relax.

We show them that at their core, they are valuable and valued. For some, it means they're not required to perform or make money for us to be seen as valued. Or, they don't need to be perfect or be physically well for us to continue to love them. We give them a new and better experience of what living in this physical world means. By our actions, we prove we are there for them through their darkest times, whether it's emotional or physical.[19]

To tell you the truth, that is why I love working with people and the animals they love. Because your love for your animal, whether they misbehave, act in ways you don't understand, or are on their way out of this life in a very messy way, reminds me that humans have the capacity to be good beings. We have the capacity for great love and compassion. Thank you for what you do and who you are for your animals.

ANIMALS ARE PART OF OUR SOUL FAMILIES

We and our animal friends share a spiritual connection, just as we do with our close friends, parents, and children. Indeed, many refer to their animals as their children, but just as our children grow and mature, so do our animal companions. I love the term to describe this spiritual connection—our "soul families."

We know that we probably will outlive our animals. In fact, most of us already have outlived our animals and experienced how the end of our animal's life is particularly difficult. Unlike our human family, it is up to us to decide when to let them go. We struggle, we cry, and we wonder if we made the right decision. Most people don't understand the level of grief we experience.

The term soul family has usually been used only with other humans. Soul families consist of more than just our close relations; they include the people we have significant relationships with, such as friends, colleagues, and others we've touched and who have touched us.

The people in our soul family incarnate together because they love each other—and they also have unresolved issues from a prior life.

I've taken this relationship a step further and hope you will take it to heart as well. I have had animals since I was a little kid, and I know this first-hand. I still remember all my long-gone animals with affection and still miss them despite knowing they are okay. I include the animals in my life as part of my soul family. It brings me comfort. Whatever your spiritual understanding, I invite you to see how you could incorporate the belief that you have a soul family, and it includes your animals, too.

I know so clearly how our animals, like our humans, have played major parts in our life story. So, I declare they're part of our soul family. And, as our soul companions, if we let them, animals can help guide and comfort us in life and in death.

This leads me to the belief that their souls are eternal, just as human souls are. They stay connected with us through eternity through the love we have for each other. Also, they choose our family again if and when they reincarnate.

ANIMALS CAN GIVE GUIDANCE EVEN AFTER THEY DIE

I've contacted animals who have given advice and have challenged their humans to take steps toward new growth. When their essence is no longer in their animal bodies, animals are able to "see" more expansively and ethereally. They can see the big picture. They don't have the same emotional attachment and reaction to their physical form and personality that they had when they were alive.

To explain a bit more, animals have a personality (the being you and I knew when they lived with us) and a Higher Self (the essence of who they are beyond that physical experience), just like people do. Their personality is attached to the animal species, and their higher self is closer to the Creator's vibration.

After the animals I've worked with have passed on, some have the ability to share a loving perspective with their human that nudges their human on their path of spiritual growth. If the human is open to their advice, they have found the information incredibly on target.

I know it seems strange that you could get good advice from an animal, but I've often experienced that, when the guardian and I reflected on what the animal shared, we agreed the information was right on target and very useful. After a few similar experiences, we begin to accept the truth that animals can be much more than a loving companion.

Now, this is not true of all animals—just as it may not be true for all humans who pass on. Their basic personality, and their level of connection to Spirit and their Higher Self, differs depending on their many experiences and how they handled them. That influences what they might share after they pass. There's no judgement here. We've all heard of "old souls" who just understand more of life and death.

My definition of an old soul is someone (human or non-human) who has made significant spiritual progress. It's not a function of how long they lived or how many times they've been around the block (for those who believe in reincarnation). It's more a function of how much they grew spiritually through the challenges presented to them. It seems to me that "old souls" may be more likely to give insight or guidance.

∾

Callie: Break Free

You'll hear more about Callie's transition later in the book, but I'd like to share the guidance she gave Mary after she transitioned. Before her transition, Callie was having episodes of unexpected violence. And that's *dangerous* when a puny human is close to a horse. I connected with Callie to find out what was happening. From my layperson's viewpoint, having dated a guy with epilepsy in my twenties, it felt like Callie was having a grand mal seizure and wasn't doing it purposefully.

I "saw" Callie kicking down the walls of her stall (it was more of a warning than a reality). So, I asked Mary to be careful. Still, Callie caught Mary's leg. Lucky for Mary, it was only a bad bruise.

After Callie passed, we reconnected. Callie had a message for Mary. She said that even as Callie had broken down the walls to her stall, Mary was going to have to break through the walls of her stall—some personal limitation—to be free.

Recently, Mary shared that she finally understood what Callie was referring to. Mary's sister had become estranged from her, and this sister literally erected barriers between them.

When Mary learned that her sister was dying, she remembered what Callie had said. So, she did whatever she had to do to break through the emotional barriers to connect to her sister. Mary re-established a loving relationship between them before her sister passed. This loss, although devastating, had one less thorn of pain to live with.

∾

Later in the book, you'll also learn more about how Mitsubishi, my dear Siberian Husky, has given me insight and advice since he passed in 2012, including how he presents himself and communicates with me. It's much different than the fun-loving, mischievous dog I knew when he was in his physical body.

4

FINDING A SPIRITUAL APPROACH
TO LOSING OUR ANIMALS

" The intellect uses only the faculties of reason, conceptu-
alization, and interpretation to translate our experiences
into a mental framework of understanding. It doesn't
help when the heart is breaking because someone close
to us has died. We must go to deeper levels of ourselves
in order to receive the healing needed.

— ROBERT J. GRANT, *THE PLACE WE CALL HOME*[20]

I CATEGORIZE our responses to our animal's death into two groups:
the personal and the spiritual. The personal response is how a death
affects us emotionally. If you only experience personal responses,
death feels devastating. All sorts of issues come up:

- Did I hold on too long?
- Did I let them go before "their time"?
- They were too young.
- How could they have died from [inset cause]? I did
  everything I knew to keep them healthy.
- I'm not ready to let them go. How will I go on?

- I'm embarrassed to admit it, but I'm a bit relieved. They were suffering and/or taking care of them was a burden.
- Why did they die when I wasn't home? Didn't they love me?
- If it was from other circumstances—predator, accident, bad food, bad medicine— Why my animal? Could I have prevented it? My grief is overwhelming me.

A SPIRITUAL UNDERSTANDING

All these strong, negative emotions are normal. However, if you spend a lot of time there, it's a recipe for homemade hell. It also puts up a barrier to reconnecting with your animal after they've passed.

Don't put aside the personal responses to death. Embrace the questions and emotions like they are small children needing comfort. Answer and honor them as best you can. Let them go when they're ready. Don't hang on to them beyond their shelf life—that is poison to your wellbeing.

Develop a spiritual response to death instead of the simply human perspective of loss and grief. I invite you—and I give you permission—to create your own spiritual reality of death. If you believe people survive death, can you extend this belief to animals? Since I've experienced my own animals' presences after they died, I know this is a reality.

You might develop a daily spiritual practice that includes your animals. Every morning, I turn my life and will over to the care of Creator. I ask that I be guided to be and do what Creator and my Higher Self have always known I'm here for. And I practice a modality that boosts the energy field for myself and my family. Of course, this includes my animals.

Developing a daily spiritual practice that includes your animals can provide some breathing space, a place of sanctuary. This may help you pull the heavy curtain of emotion aside so you can see your animal's viewpoint: what they're experiencing and what they desire. It roots you into a quieter place with less distraction.

HOW DO YOU RECONCILE YOURSELF TO LOSING SOMEONE YOU LOVE?

You might start with your version of my belief that "Creator doeth all things well." I see our lives are like beautiful woven blankets or baskets. Creator takes all the twists and turns of our lives—the experiences, feelings, all of it—and weaves each life into a deeply moving and beautiful work of art. There are gifts for everyone who's open to them. Creator can offer meaning and purpose for the one who died and the ones who love them.

CLEAR OUT YOUR "BAGGAGE"

Clearing out your own thoughts, beliefs, and assumptions about your animal leaves room to see them as separate beings with their own personalities, preferences, and peculiarities. We can more easily see if they want to continue or they're ready to go. We can even accept when they change their minds.

This is so useful, but difficult because we are incredibly attached to our animals. What beliefs and thoughts about what's happening to your animal are you holding on to that no longer serve you?

If you can keep this question in mind, it may help you navigate through the last part of their life. When you recognize your own needs and desires in the relationship, acknowledge them. There's nothing wrong with your feelings. Look into your heart, and from your heart space, you will remember that you want what's best for your animal.

STOP BEING THE FIXER

One underlying, unconscious belief is that it's your responsibility to fix your animals and to bring them back to health. May I be blunt? With an abundance of compassion, it seems as if you believe you're God in this situation. If you just find the right doctor, treatment, and energy healing, it will all work out.

Let me be clear: I am not saying give up or don't try. There are so many modalities out there. One of them may be the answer to helping your animal heal so you both get to spend more time together. But please take yourself off the hook *now*.

If you continue to believe that you're an almighty powerful being who can bring your animals back to health, it will bite you in the butt after your animal passes on. I've heard it from loving, decent people. They feel they failed their animal because they didn't do enough. They didn't find the cure that was right around the corner.

As far as I know, we all die eventually, including your beloved animal. I can almost hear you say, "Yes, of course, I know that!" But deep down, we deny it for as long as we can. It's so hard to bear this truth. So, you give yourself this heavy mission, and at some point, you will fail at achieving your mission. Your animals will pass on into spirit.

Stop being the fixer. Surround yourself with self-love. Acknowledge you're human. As a human, you will probably be unable to keep your loved ones alive for the entire time you're on the planet. Instead of believing you will prevail over all odds, shift to a softer, more comforting belief.

Tell yourself you'll do all you can to help your animal stay in their body until it doesn't make sense anymore. That's about the time no one's having fun. Remember, it isn't the end. Animals, like humans, survive death. Releasing them from their physical body can be a blessing for them. They will be grateful once they feel the pleasure of being whole again in the spiritual plane. I guarantee it.

~

Tug and Jazz: No More Fixing, Mom!
A wonderful client, Laurence, shared about trying to be the fixer:

> When we got our two Labradors Retrievers almost 12 years
> ago, I had already been focused on nourishing food and exercise
> for a very long time for our family. So, it was easy to include

Jazz and Tug. We got Jazz as a male puppy and Tug as a seven-year-old female. They were both our first pets.

It is only recently, after a session with Maribeth, that I painfully realized that being obsessed with their health has robbed me of the most beautiful part of my relationship with my two beautiful dogs: the soul connection, the fun, the freedom.

Tug died at fifteen with numerous health issues that should have led to a much earlier euthanasia. I wanted her to heal and die on her own. I could not make the decision to euthanize her until our vet explained to me how difficult her life was.

Jazz started to show lameness in his back legs a while ago, and again I was trying to find a healing; I desperately wanted perfect health for him no matter his age. Our vets cannot find anything obvious, and he doesn't show signs of pain. He is still active and enthusiastic.

After the session with Maribeth, I let go. I discovered that I was missing out on the soul connection with Jazz because I was so driven and focused on "doing the right thing" for his body, feeling over responsible about it and like a failure if I couldn't find a solution. This was a lot for me to carry around, and it got in the way of our relationship.

I now deeply enjoy our time together, so relaxed and fun, just being with each other. I can see how precious this time of his life is: the adorable senior dog that smells every blade of grass and doesn't care about exercise (but as a lab cares a lot about food!).

It is amazing that he still walks a significant distance every day, but he decides where, when, and at what pace. We now walk behind him!

I realize now the weight, one of "fighting disease so I could keep him longer," was a heavy one. Now, I am going with the flow, accepting that aging can be a beautiful time of life, even if the body is not perfect. I am accepting that his life span is much shorter than ours and that one day he won't be with us anymore (I am not sure I have completely accepted this one yet...)

Laurence and Jazz. Photo credit: Laurence Martin.

∿

It is amazing how much our pets teach us about ourselves and about life.

PRACTICE NONJUDGMENT AND COMPASSION

Truth talk again. When our animals start to deteriorate, we are taken aback. Intellectually we knew this time would come. But now? No, it's too early. And if you tell yourself the truth, you find it annoying at times. We've got a life that works. They have their roles, and we have ours. Not to mention how worried we become as our animals age. Here are some of the questions I've experienced as my animals aged:

- Why are they peeing and pooping where they know they shouldn't?

- She used to love walks. Now we walk so slow, I'm not sure I should call it a walk. A creep? A sniff fest?
- I don't think they can hear me. Or I'm not sure they can see so well.
- What's that lump and why is it getting bigger?
- Why are they limping?
- He's so cranky lately. Could he be in pain?
- She won't eat anything unless I hand feed her.

And then we begin to wonder if we should take our animals to the veterinarian. I tend to wait and hope it just goes away on its own because I don't want to hear bad news. Most of us get them to the veterinarian sooner or later. That's because we love them. You may have another way of coping with this deterioration.

Please work to see yourself and your animals with nonjudgment and compassion during this time. You're both having a hard time coping with this new reality. Be gentle, take a breath, and remember the love you have for them. And appreciate that you are opening the door to a reality you don't want. But, because you love them, you will.

Take time to manage your own energy and state of mind. By managing your own energy, you should re-experience your love for them at this moment. Dig into your desire to serve them as long as they're with you. Forgive yourself for losing your patience or being afraid of doing the next right thing for them. Figure out ways to live with this new reality.

REMEMBER: THEY'RE NOT DEAD YET!

I wrote, "Hey, Human! I'm not dead yet!" as my lovely dog Stella's physical abilities started declining. It's a reminder to stay in the now. Stop projecting forward to things getting worse. They likely will decline. But, focusing on future bad outcomes tends to ruin any current happy moments you can still have with your animals.

"I'm not dead yet!" is one of my favorite scenes from the movie, *Monty Python and the Holy Grail*.[21] The film was set during the

Black Plague in England. It's the kind of grim humor I love to snicker at (although it's definitely *NOT* a lesson in compassionate human behavior).

"I'm not dead yet!" is a great phrase to remember when our animals get older. I hear some version of this sentiment when I have sessions with many animals who are getting older. Almost always, they address the sadness their human has about their loss of abilities.

∼

Joe: Not Dead Yet

Sara was concerned about her horse Joe's low energy. We talked about what was bumming Joe out and how Sara could help. Part of what was bumming Joe out was Sara's sadness over Joe's decline. Afterward, Sara emailed me to say:

Joe. Photo credit: Sara B.

After our talk in February with my thirty-year-old horse Joe, he certainly did perk up! Our agreements (discussions) worked—he shares more [supportive] energy as long as I bring happier energy.

As the weather has warmed up, we have been playing more often. Joe even started jumping while we are playing on the ground! Imagine that! A half-blind horse with some mobility limitations enjoying jumping!

After he showed me that he likes bareback, we've been doing bareback rides once or twice a week for the last two weeks. He even cantered last Saturday!

Today we were riding in the pasture and found a bunch of groundhog holes and had to move spaces where the boys (horses) were living. Joe helped me move everyone in and work the gate just like the old days!

Thank you for helping us to make sure we are both getting what we need and assure me that Joe is still just as fun and spunky as ever.

∽

Stella Lives!

Stella's hearing and eyesight had diminished significantly. At one point, we thought Stella had lost her spark.

Stella. Photo credit: Maribeth Decker.

The veterinarian checked her out and reported nothing has worsened, which was good news. We adjusted the CBD oil for joint pain, and our holistic veterinarian prescribed herbal medicines to help her "sparkiness" return (yes, I just invented a word, and I'm proud of it).

We, as her human companions, had to adjust *our* attitudes to help reignite Stella's sparkiness. We worked to exude the "Stella's not dead yet" attitude. With our change in attitude, we adjusted our behaviors, including how we talked to her. Here's what happened:

- I noticed Stella would walk much faster off leash, but then she got lost. So, I found some narrow, safe paths at two local parks where she could trot behind Tibor and me. Her open grin while walking off leash made my day. I still had to check on her, but we figured out how to make it fun for all of us!

- Stella used to love snuggling on the bed with us just before the lights when out. But she couldn't jump up and wouldn't use a ramp or stairs. She stopped trying to come up. To remedy this, I called excitedly, "Stella, do you want to come up on the bed?" If she wanted to come up, she'd put her front paws on the bed, clearly saying, "Yes, I would! Lift me up, please!" She began spending more time on the bed again!

- My husband and I reached out to touch her and talk to her more often. We invited her to join us wherever we were hanging out.

- I worked to find my patient person when I took her out on a walk. This way, I didn't exude impatience and irritation at her slowness. Honestly, it was very difficult transition from my "we're here for exercise!!" mentality.

- Tibor and I took "sneaky walks" without Stella so he and I could still get in a brisk walk.

- Finally, we told Stella about how happy and blessed we were to have her in our life. We shared with her what joy her personality brought to the family.

I didn't know how long Stella would be with us as that's not my specialty, but I felt good about how we worked through this time of her life.

~

FINDING PEACE WHEN WE DECIDE TO EUTHANIZE

Since we have the option to euthanize our animals, we have the added responsibility/burden of deciding whether to let them go. It helps if we can know their desires—if they are ready to move on.

As your animal's guardian, you may have to decide to let them go, but that's okay. When they joined your family, they gave you a spiritual medical power of attorney so you can make medical decisions for them.

We know they can't say to the veterinarian, "Yes, I'll go through that procedure. I have the stamina and desire to live!" Or, "I'm tired. No more procedures, let's move on to a peaceful finish." Instead, on a spiritual level, they look to you to make the right decision for them.

So, we notice their lives, their quality of life. What fun things can they still do? Are they eating and drinking? Can they walk, run, or play? How much physical discomfort are they in? Can you make it better through medication, medical intuition or energy healing sessions, animal communications sessions, herbs, acupuncture, or massage?

Still, at some point, you realize more medical interaction isn't helping and their physical condition is worsening. It's tough when you sense they don't realize the gravity of their situation. So, you'll need to explain how they may start feeling a lot worse if you don't release them from their body. That's because you want to spare them that discomfort.

I strongly believe our animals consented to you being their guardians and caretakers. They chose you as much as you chose them. They said, "You're my human. Take care of me the best you can. I know you'll make the right decision. I trust you."

Your decisions don't have to be perfect. There is rarely a straight path from taking care of a healthy soul to caretaking a soul whose body is weakening. Instead of perfection, you are called to make each decision with pure love. In pure love, ask, "What's best for my animal right now?" And, "What can I do to acknowledge my feelings so I make the best decision for them?"

Check out the Resources section of this book for an excellent checklist, "How Do I Know When it's Time?" from The Ohio State University's Veterinary Medical Center. It may help you assess your animal's quality of life from a more grounded position.

Release your need to make the perfect decision. Trust that your love was the best balm for your animal's transition—they knew they were and *are still* loved. And if it works for you, believe that Creator helps smooth the transition and there are friends and family on the other side helping, too.

REALIZE ANIMALS SOMETIMES CHECK OUT LIFE ON THE OTHER SIDE

Some animals know there's another realm, an afterlife for them to continue their existence. That can make the transition easier for them when we let them go.

I've met cats and dogs who were "checking out" the other side before they left. One cat would disappear outside for a longer period of time than usual because she was able to sense the other side when she was outside. She would always return home, but this was her way of preparing herself for the transition.

Other cats and dogs are in such a deep, almost trance-like sleep, their people are afraid they've died. Their humans softly touch them to see if they respond and then realize they're still breathing. I would imagine their human just gave a heavy sigh of relief! The information I've received is their animals are visiting the "world" they'll be going to when their body gives out.

DISCONNECTION EXPLORATION

My friend Pete has some extraordinary psychic abilities, and so I shared with him that I felt my dog Stella was in the process of visiting the other realm He explained it so beautifully:

> As you are aware, our kids and animals grow and expand their consciousness and understanding in direct consequence of being near us. It can't be helped. As I read your lines about Stella, I felt a "stretched cord," a bungee cord under pressure— which, from my work, signifies "Disconnection Exploration." Unless I am missing something, nothing felt imminent, but I would lean towards the thought that Stella is exploring what it would mean to her and everyone else whenever she does pass.

> You did exactly as you should with telling her it was okay. When I had a sense that Dewey, our last Basset Hound, was considering the possibilities [of transitioning], I told him something to the effect that, "Dewey, I can't imagine how frustrating it must feel to be wearing a diaper or not being able to get up on the couch or run around with Val (our other dog) anymore. When you feel you have accomplished all you needed to do here, I want you to know we will support your decision to leave the physical. We would never want you to be in pain or to be in the physical any longer than you would want or are comfortable or feel fulfilled.

> My point is I am a firm believer that our animals can explore the meaning of their death far more than we realize.

NOT ALL OUR ANIMALS ARE CLEAR ABOUT WHAT'S UP NEXT

Unlike those animals who check out "the other side," some of our animals may not be sure what's next. When they feel done, worn out, and they don't (or can't) find pleasure anymore in what they used to enjoy, they may welcome release from their bodies when they understand that there's another option.

You know your animal. Ask yourself, what makes his or her life worth living? Is your animal finding no or little pleasure in activities that used to be fun? Is your animal eating? Other things to look for are incontinence, memory issues, or crying, yelping, or growling when you try to help move them. These are all signs it might be the time to say good-bye.

It's more than just your animal being ready to go. It's also about you and your human family being ready to let your animal go. I think we, the guardians of our animals, should start with an intention to make decisions for the animal's highest good within the limits of what we are capable of providing logistically. There may be a limit to what can we afford for their care and whether we're capable of caring for them properly. Maybe more importantly, we may also find that our hearts can only bear so much.

With that said, don't be hasty. There are many options a good veterinarian can recommend. And there are so many additional therapies to explore. Get good advice. Then let your heart and clear intention guide you.

My dogs have always loved walks, cuddling, and good treats. In the mid-1980s while stationed in Hawaii, my husband and I adopted a poi dog off the streets that we named Missy. She was an incredibly active dog, and I loved running with her, in part because I could always count on her to pull (drag?) me up a steep hill if I lagged behind. Her strength and dynamic "leadership" were awesome.

In her final year, though, Missy couldn't move easily. She sat on the couch in our house in Virginia, and I had to hand feed her because she couldn't get up the stairs to her food bowl. I thought, "Oh, no, this it! This is the end!" But, it wasn't. My vet provided some good medications to manage what turned out to be a lot of pain. Missy perked right back up, and we gained a few more wonderful years.

CONSIDER THE TIMING OF THEIR PASSING AS PART OF THEIR SPIRITUAL JOURNEY

If you allow the belief that animals might have a spiritual journey separate from yours, it may help you find peace. The Buddhists believe that all sentient beings—which includes animals—have the ability to achieve enlightenment. So do I.

So, when our animals disappear from our lives before we're ready, our role is to support them, providing love and guidance. That includes letting them go when the time is right or accepting that they left exactly when the time was right for them. In the story of their life, we may have a leading role, chapter, paragraph, or be mentioned in a footnote. It's not solely about us. Rather humbling.

5

THE TIMING OF THEIR DEATH IS TRICKY

66 And we wept that one so lovely should have a life so brief.

— WILLIAM CULLEN BRYANT

GROWING UP, I heard people say, "When it's your time to go, it's your time to go." Those people believed our ending was set in stone, which can be a comforting thought when we lose our animals. It relieves us of guilt over what we did or didn't do for them. Their time was up, period. But my work with animals as they age has led me to a bit more complicated story of endings. I think animals and Creator work together to decide when they'll leave the planet. We are part of the decision, but we're supporting actors in their life story.

THE CAPITAL BELTWAY—A WAY OF SEEING LIFE

I received the oddest "download" as a way to understand the timing of our animals' deaths—driving the Capital Beltway! I've been driving the beltway since I moved to Northern Virginia in the early 1990s to serve my last tour of duty in the Navy. So, I've had a lot of experience watching driving habits.

The Capital Beltway is a sixty-four-mile, eight-to-ten lane highway that circles Washington, D.C. It passes through Virginia and Maryland. There are exits every few miles. Many times, you can make great time driving around, but other times you inch your way along.

Moving towards the end of life seems like deciding which exit to take on the Capital Beltway. There's not just one exit point. Instead, animals have choices regarding which exit to take. All exits lead back to Spirit, to release of pain, reunion with loved ones, and knowing they were cherished.

For many years, our animals have been driving in the fast or middle lane on the proverbial beltway. At some point, we realize they seem to drift off into the slow lane. They start moving back and forth between the middle and slow lanes. Their bodies slow down; they begin to work less efficiently than they used to.

What's lovely about this stage is that we can still help them "gas back up" or "get a tune-up." In car terms, their engine, electrical system, and suspension are still in good enough working order to be kept running. From the body's perspective, good medical care (western, holistic, and alternative) and a useful attitude on our part make a huge difference. Good medical care addresses the body's needs to function better, or just maintain speed and lessen pain.

A useful attitude for us is to focus on finding gratitude for whatever they're still able to do. This gratitude positively affects *their* quality of life. For instance, we can be grateful for each and every day we get to be with them. As a result, we sometimes become more willing to readjust our lives, when possible, to meet their needs.

Some animals move into the slow land and start driving under the speed limit as they physically decline. Their body seems to be running out of gas. Or, in spiritual terms, the life force—the spirit or energy that animates living creatures or the soul—is slowly leaving the body.This is a time when interventions that worked before don't perk them up. They're not looking to refuel (eat and drink) anymore. In fact, their engines (circulation, nervous system, digestive system) seem to be shutting down.

Those animals seek the nearest exit. Sometimes they want to choose their own exit. But, if they're physically uncomfortable, euthanasia feels like a good decision to help release them from their pain and suffering.

ARE THEY READY TO GO?

This is where it gets tricky for us. At times, we're sure this is it. Our animals have been in the slow lane, and we see them eyeing a couple of exits through their behavior.

But, suddenly they perk up and start enjoying life again: eating and moving with that spark of life back in their eye. They drove by the exit instead of taking one. "Nope. Not this one." They might even move into the middle lane and almost get back up to the speed limit!

You may notice a change in behavior when you've been able to soothe their pain. Remember my amazement and delight when my dog Missy sprang back to life when she received medication for her arthritis?

Sometimes we receive strong and clear messages that our animals are in the slow lane and thinking about exiting. I hope the following stories gives you a sense of wonder about animal transitions.

Stop and think deeply with your family about what is next when you are faced with that decision. Quality of life—yours and theirs—is usually the decider. Don't forget to check with a good healthcare provider to see if pain or other symptoms can be managed.

If the options you are given by your healthcare provider are too difficult for you to manage without turning your world around or aren't guaranteed to help the animal extend their quality of life, then hospice care should be considered until the end time is clear. Or, if it is time, a good ending is a merciful choice.

Please note that I am not suggesting you withhold reasonable care for manageable chronic issues, accidents, or if you can afford it, surgery. Animal guardians have a sacred trust to care for the animals in their lives as best they can—ensuring their quality of life is part of that trust.

WATCH FOR CHANGES

The bottom line is that the day and time your animals pass isn't set in stone. Notice in which lane your animal is driving in on the Beltway of Life. Here are some questions to ask yourself as you watch them decline.

- If they're moving in and out of the slow lane, what can you do tune them up? How can you support them emotionally?
- If they are driving under the speed limit in the slow lane and checking out the exits, how can you make them comfortable?
- Are there signs that their body is shutting down?
- Does it feel like the exit offers more quality of life than the slow lane?

Ashley: Not Quite Yet

My colleague and friend Gail had an Australian Shepherd, fifteen-and-a-half-year-old Ashley, who had serious health problems like osteosarcoma. Gail took Ashley regularly to the vet for more than nine months. It was possible Ashley might not survive, but she was a fighter and continuously rallied even though she was in

Ashley. Photo credit: Gail S.

her advanced years. Ashley and Gail were soulmates and had been together through thick and thin.

At one point while on a business trip, Gail received daily telephone reports about Ashley's condition. Gail knew Ashley was getting tired of fighting her battle, and her strength was declining. As Gail and I talked during the business meeting, it became clear to me that Ashley would hang in there until Gail returned home and made peace with Ashley's upcoming transition. Gail returned home to Ashley, and they spent three weeks of quality time together while Gail prepared herself for Ashley's inevitable passing.

On the day of Ashley's passing, Gail woke up knowing it was time to let Ashley transition in peace and no longer be in pain. Gail believed Ashley gave her permission and everything would be okay. I was moved by Ashley's willingness to endure serious physical distress to spend time "in the flesh" with Gail before passing away. This time was a gift to Gail and made Ashley happy.

To this day, Gail can often feel Ashley's presence and sometimes even hear her while Gail's working in her office.

~

Buster: Nope!

Photo credit: Tara Lynn and Co.,
Shutterstock.

A client had brought home a puppy to add to their family. They already had an older boxer, Buster. Buster had cancer and behavioral issues. The client wondered if Buster was ready to transition. The information I received was, no.

Buster thought his family planned to get rid of him. He reasoned there always had been only one dog in the house and now there were two. Somebody had to go—and it looked like he was the most likely candidate! He definitely wasn't ready to transition, but he felt agitated.

Truthfully, the family had brought in the puppy to ease the transition when Buster was ready to go, and Buster picked up on it. However, his family loved Buster and were in no hurry to experience the ending.

I assured Buster they were not going to get rid of him. I told him he had a role in teaching the puppy the rules of the house. When Buster was ready to go, his symptoms very clearly indicated to his family it was time.

On a side note, Buster showed me animals have a sense of humor. The puppy was yapping incessantly, and I thought, "Boy, that is one noisy little dog."

I immediately heard a response from Buster, who said, "There are some advantages to losing your hearing when you get older."

~

Myron: I'm so ready!

Keiko and Dan had so much love for their dog, Myron, who had a number of serious and chronic issues. Keiko and Dan made sure that Myron received the best medical care. They looked for and tried all the newest treatments for Myron.

I met them at the Veterinary Holistic Center in Springfield, Virginia. They wanted to know how strong Myron's desire was to continue to stay in his body. They had found a wonderful cutting-edge treatment program in Ohio that sounded encouraging.

"What does Myron think of a trip to Ohio for this new treatment?" they asked me.

When I connected to Myron, he felt tired and worn out. I showed him the travel to Ohio, and asked if he'd like to do that to get better. His response was a clear no.

I thought about how to share this news with Keiko and Dan in a compassionate way. What if Myron was my dog? How would I want to hear this news? I explained Myron's weariness and discomfort, and that it was overriding his love for being with them. Then I said that no, he did not want to go to Ohio. He did not want any more treatment. He wanted peace.

They were good people and wanted what was best for Myron. So, they were ready to accept his desires and allow him to decline his own way.

The next day, Keiko called me with some tough news. Myron had

had a heart attack and did not survive the night. I wondered how she felt and worried our conversation might be challenging. Instead, it turned out to be a wonderful conversation. Having a background in energy healing, Keiko felt that once Myron had communicated with his people what he desired, he finally could let go. They felt peace that, in this case, they did not have to make the decision.

~

Summer: Thanks, I'm Ready Now

When Sarah contacted me, her distress was clear. Her beloved pug Summer, who had dealt with cancer for some time, was finally giving up. Even though it was the Fourth of July, I made time to do an emergency session. For me, Summer was as much of a friend as Sarah. Being there for friends feels right to me—even on a holiday.

Summer. Photo credit: Sarah L.

I checked in with Summer, and felt she was physically uncomfortable and emotionally worn out. Both Summer and Sarah needed to say goodbye. So, I facilitated that conversation. We told Summer what to expect and how to let go of her body. Sarah was able to let Summer go the next day, feeling they said what needed to be said to let each other move on.

~

Gustav: I'm Not Going to Tell You I'm Ready

You remember Gustav the Bernese Mountain Dog standing next to the Pope in a photograph earlier in this book? Liz asked me to do a session with him as he was losing weight and their veterinarian was not sure why. She wasn't concerned that Gustav was ready to transition, only if I could provide more information about his condition.

When I connected with Gustav, I did not find anything specific other than he was very dehydrated. (Just to be clear, I am not a veterinarian and do not diagnose illnesses; but I can provide useful information in addition to what vets are providing my clients.)

Shortly afterward, Gustav was diagnosed with lymphoma and pancreatitis. They started treatment, which seemed to be going well for a day or two, but then he crashed with vomiting and diarrhea. He was finally diagnosed with systemic inflammatory response syndrome (SIRS). They were unable to save him.

I felt rattled and saddened by his sudden passing and asked my animal communication teacher to check in on Gustav to see what happened. She told me he had hidden the extent of his illness from all of us because he was ready to transition. He did not want to go through treatment and did not want his family to suffer, either.

I later asked Gustav about it, and he affirmed that my teacher was right. Liz shared the information with Gustav's veterinarians, and she reported it provided them with some comfort.

∽

Since Gustav, I've met more animals who have "hidden" their disease diagnosis from the people and veterinarians. If you receive a diagnosis so late that treatment options are limited or non-existent, know that something spiritual is in play. Your animal, on a spiritual level, did not want you to know about the illness. It saved you months or years of distraught management. And, it saved them from medical treatments that would be involved. These decisions are made at the soul level, not the conscious level.

∽

Callie: Seizures and Arthritis

I first worked with Callie when her seizures and arthritis caused issues. The energetic healing gave her additional time on the earth, but she was about eighteen years old. A few years later, she began having unexpected outbursts of kicking and biting, which endangered her horse friend, Izzy, and her guardian, Mary. So, I was asked to see what was happening.

Callie with Maribeth.

When I contacted Callie, she had no memory of the outbursts. She let me experience what she was experiencing, and it seemed like she was in a trance during those outbursts. I'm not a veterinarian, but I would call the outbursts violent epileptic seizures.

Once she understood what was happening, she was definitely ready to go. She worried she might hurt her family. In fact, I "saw" her knock me down and step on me. I warned Mary about that vision because I worried Mary might get hurt. Sure enough, Callie did kick Mary shortly afterward. Luckily, the kick was in the thigh so, while Mary was sore, there was no real damage.

When it was time to go, I explained to Callie that she'd go out in the pasture with the veterinarian and Mary. Callie could just step out of her body when her body stopped breathing. Mary reported Callie happily trotted into the pasture to meet the vet. There was no drama. Her horse friend, Izzy, stuck her head out of the barn window at the moment Callie passed and neighed. Izzy is very intuitive and knew what had happened.

∽

Emma: Closed for Business

Jill asked me to check on Emma, her warm and wonderful basset hound. Was she ready to go? Emma's body was winding down, but her spirit was strong. She told me she wanted to continue with Jill. When I checked her physical condition, though, her digestive system showed me a sign that said, "Closed for business." And, it wasn't opening back up—this was a permanent closure.

I shared this information with Jill and Emma. We explained to Emma that her body couldn't do anything with food anymore, and she

was going to become more uncomfortable. With Jill's permission, we explained that Jill was going to release Emma from her body so she could feel well and perky again. Jill loved her immensely and didn't want Emma to suffer.

Jill was with Emma and her transition was easy (for Emma). I believe Jill was comforted by knowing Emma understood the reason for Jill's decision.

Emma. Photo credit: Jill Celeste.

6

ANIMAL COMMUNICATION STRATEGIES

❝ Welcome to Telepathics' Anonymous. Don't bother introducing yourself.

— M.C. HUMPHRIES BAUVARD, *SOME INSPIRATION FOR THE OVERENTHUSIASTIC*

As YOU KNOW, I'm often asked to help people navigate their animal's transition (that's why I wrote this book!). In this chapter, I'll share some of my strategies in case you'd like to try your hand at animal communication.

The best animal communication, for me, starts with a heart connection, a sense of love or compassion for the being you want to connect with. From that loving place, intuition flows. So here's the good news: You're already connected to your animal emotionally or you wouldn't be reading this book.

Build on this love to intuitively send to and receive information from them. Ask questions verbally and assume they understand what you're saying. If you are able, imagine pictures in your head that pertain to what you're asking. Believe you are sharing those pictures with your animal as you ask the question. Trust and try.

Very important! Before you connect intuitively, see if you're filled with worry, dread, or sadness. That's so normal. If you are, stop, shake it off (dog people know what I mean!). and then fill your heart with love and appreciation for your animal. Replace your worry with heart-felt love. This will help you receive the answer.

ACCEPT THE FIRST PIECE OF INFORMATION THAT SHOWS UP

The first thought, picture, emotion, or physical feeling that shows up is usually communication from your animal. After that, your logical mind takes over. You can always ask your animal if you got it right, and listen for a yes or no. If you need to, take a break, re-center yourself in love, then ask them your question again.

CHECK THEIR LIFE FORCE

You may be able to intuitively check their life force—called Chi, Ki, or Prana (universal energy that flows in currents in and around the body). Life force is what animates the body. Without it, the body is lifeless.

As we all age, we have less life force. Ask how much life force is in their body. When you connect with your animals, be open to experiencing their response in your own way. Here are some ways I have received a response.

- On a scale of 0-100%, how much life force is left? In my experience, less than 30% usually means you should focus on keeping them comfortable. They're in the slow lane.
- How sparkly is it when you imagine you're looking inside their body? If it's pretty dark, probably the slow lane. If you see more sparkles, anticipate more movement between the middle and slow lanes.
- You get a symbolic representation. For instance, when I checked in with my son's dog, Peanut, I felt like I was

looking at a ghost town. Think of the symbolism of a ghost town: The physical structure was still there, but the people (the life of the town) were not. At that point, I felt Peanut was definitely in the slow lane, and it was time to create an exit strategy for her.

Please don't use life force solely to predict how long they'll stay in their body. What it *will* do is give you an idea of how to choose or focus your medical interventions or energy healing efforts. Is the primary purpose to bring the body back to better health, or to bring it comfort as it slows down and starts looking for the right exit?

IF YOU'RE UP TO IT, ASK IF THEY'RE READY TO GO

If you don't ask, you won't know. People discount information so often. Give your animal a chance to connect on this important subject.

QUESTIONS TO ASK TO HELP YOU DECIDE

There are certain questions you can ask your animal to help you understand if they're ready, such as:

- Do you want more medical procedures so you can stay with us? How about medicines? At a certain point, most living beings just want to pass in peace with no more intrusive procedures, or without more induced pain to keep them in their bodies.
- How physically comfortable are you? Your eyes might be drawn to a part of their body as a way of telling you it hurts. You might even feel pain in a place that the doctor has told you is a problem spot. That might be an indication to adjust medication.
- What do you still enjoy? In many cases, you'll get a fleeting picture of something that you do for them or they like to do by themselves. Honor it.

- What can I do to make your life more enjoyable? Ask them
  —more cuddle time, play time, special treats, music, or
  being outside even if they can't walk much?
- Is there something you want to do before you pass on?

Keep in mind your animal may send this information to you in many ways. Don't discount what you receive. You may hear something (maybe a song if that's your jam), feel an emotion, or experience a physical sensation. A memory might pop in and, if so, think about what that memory means in your life. You might see them with wings or running free in a meadow. If you're not sure what this information means, tell them you're not sure you understand. Ask them to use human words.

Sometimes they offer a "yes"—they're not having fun, they're in a lot of pain, they're tired of being alive, or they don't want any more medical interventions. If they do say yes, you can explain that they can leave their body before it starts to shut down. Just step out of it when the time is right.

ASK FOR A SIGN WHEN THEY ARE READY

You can ask your animals to give you a sign when they've had enough. Things like:

- "That look."
- They touch you in a certain way to let you know they're done.
- Previously uncuddly animals suddenly become a Velcro dog/cat (or a very cuddly animal seems distant).

One of the dogs I worked with wasn't quite ready to go, but he was nearing the end and knew it. Through me, his person asked him to tell her when the dog was ready. She reported back to me that one day she woke up and went to check on how her pup was doing. He gave her a look and communicated that he was ready. She had no doubts and made the arrangements.

Pete Johnson shared:

I remember when I sat with Dewey, our last basset hound, and we explored what the Rainbow Bridge was, who would be on the other side, and all the smells, food, and fun he would have whenever he was ready to cross it. Not long afterwards, I put his food bowl down in the morning and clearly heard, "I'm ready."

Dewey still, on occasion shows up around Val's dog bowl, but since you spoke with Val about it, Val will jump back but continue eating.

Sometimes, despite all odds, your animals want to keep going. An older dog's response was so sweet, she made me smile. When I asked how he was feeling and if he was ready to pass, he told me that "yes" he had aches and pains, but that he was doing okay. The dog said he could handle it, and he was still interested in hanging out with their family.

If you can honor their wishes to stay on the planet, that's wonderful! But, if you see that the physical pain's getting worse for them, tell them they're going to feel worse if they stay in their body and you love them too much to let them go through that.

7

MODALITIES BEYOND REGULAR MEDICAL CARE

66 There's a popular saying among doctors: There's no such thing as alternative medicine; if it works, it's just called medicine.

— ED YONG, *I CONTAIN MULTITUDES: THE MICROBES WITHIN US AND A GRANDER VIEW OF LIFE*

IF YOUR ANIMAL IS DECLINING, here are potential strategies beyond good medical care that may help you navigate this difficult time. These practices may provide more life force energy for your animal and improve their quality of life for a longer period of time.

NOTICE WHEN LESS IS MORE

When animals spend most of their time in the slow lane of life, "less is more" can be true with medical interventions. There comes a point in an animal's life that they are *done* with poking, prodding, and seeing just one more specialist. They feel tired and worn out. They love us, but they wish we'd stop. All they want is to be made comfortable and surrounded by the people and animals who love them.

If they were human, you'd think it was time for hospice—and you'd be right. Your greatest gift to them is comfort and love at this stage. Don't forget the resource in the back of the book from The Ohio State University's Veterinary School that helps people determine their animal's enjoyment of life. It is so helpful because it's hard for us to "go there" by ourselves. As we check where our animal lands on the chart, we have data to assist us in deciding what's best for our animal.

INCREASE TENDER, FOCUSED PHYSICAL TOUCH

What's the most frequent question I hear from my clients about their ailing animals? They want to know what they can do to make their animals more comfortable. As an animal lover, I am so happy to hear this question. Even though they are filled with grief of pending loss, they focus on their animal's wellbeing.

According to the animals I've worked with, they want physical contact. So, I recommend touching your ailing animals purposefully. Think of yourself as a "therapy person" for your animal. Touch them with the idea of relieving any stress they have about how they're feeling. Your touch also will relieve stress they may be experiencing due to your sadness. Increased stress amplifies the experience of pain. Conversely, relieving their stress may decrease their physical experience of pain. There are many reports on stress and pain you can review to verify this.[22]

Think about how they respond. Watch their reactions. You already know them, so you will be able to tell what they enjoy and want more of. Do that and more.

As often as you can stand it, don't multi-task when you're providing physical affection. Let this time be just you and them. No streaming, chatting with another human on the phone, Facebook, Instagram, YouTube, Snapchat, or TikTok. Be fully present, in love with who they are.

Change your daily routine if you need to. For animals who live in the house, seek them out when you are home. Spend time sitting next to them so some part of you is touching. Snuggle if they like that.

For ailing animals who live outside the home, see how you and other humans in your family can be with them more often. Let them show you how they'd like to spend their time with you. No matter what you do together, your focused presence is extremely comforting.

Be sure to tell your ailing animals you love them and what you love about their amazing personalities! Mention how glad you are that they're still with you. Thank their ailing bodies for housing their spirit so you can enjoy another day with them.

Your focused touch comforts them (and you). It supports whatever life force energy they still have. It also supports the medical treatment you're providing because they're feeling loved.

MASSAGE

Massage therapy positively affects the animal's body and psyche. We hear about arthritis as a problem for our aging animals, but we don't hear about muscle and fascia tightness. As a licensed massage therapist for people, I am so surprised that the topic of muscle flexibility and strength isn't discussed more.

If you pay attention to your animals' non-verbal reactions, you can figure out what makes them happy and joyful. Gently working on their muscles and fascia can ease aches and improve flexibility, which improves their quality of life.

Plus, they *love* it! More accurately, my animals actually beg for a massage. Tibor shows me his neck as if to say, "Hey, do that thing you do! I love it!" Mitsubishi would lie on his back and stick out a back leg at me, clearly saying, "Get to work! Got muscles that need help!"

Massage is good for them (heck! it's also good for us). My dogs Tibor and Stella are getting up in years, but still climb the stairs and enjoy walks, although at a slower pace. That's because flexible muscles increase mobility and decrease joint pain.

I am gingerly trying out more massage with my cats Shadow, Bunnie, and Mac. They love their neck massages, so we'll see where we go next. I've been able to get a bit of shoulders massaged, and gentle ear touches are working, too. Patience is a virtue with cats!

Dr. Michael W. Fox' books *The Healing Touch for Cats*[23] and *The Healing Touch for Dogs*[24], are excellent resources, which I found useful and clear. You can learn some easy massage techniques good for dogs, cats, and other animals from his books. Dr. Fox shares the following benefits of massage:

- Helps discover trouble spots on your animal's body. We might find infections, painful spots, or growths that might need a veterinarian's care.
- Assists those suffering from impaired heart or kidney function
- Enhances postoperative recovery
- Acts as a catalyst for convalescence from sickness
- Can be added to intensive care for animals in shock and who are severely debilitated
- Deepens your bond with your animal

There are massage therapists and physical therapists for animals, many of whom will come to your home. You can also find them in a holistic veterinary office. If you use therapists like these for your animal, expect to do so on a regular basis to get the most of their unique brilliance. Be sure to ask them to show you techniques you can do at home.

TELLINGTON TTOUCH®

Tellington TTouch is a deceptively simple technique that anyone can learn. It allows your animal to switch its autonomic nervous system response from the sympathetic response (stress) to the parasympathetic response (peace). You can use TTouch for yourself, too!

TTouch isn't an energy healing technique, though. Energy healing brings in outside energy (Prana, Ki, Chi, or life force energy) to a being to assist in releasing, lightening up, or bolstering energy. TTouch® does not bring in outside energy into bodies. This is why it's not considered energy healing.

TTouch teaches people to gently move the skin in a circle and a quarter. If you picture an old-fashioned round clock face, you can envision the motion easier. First, place one hand on your animal's body to ask them to stay still for a bit. Notice this isn't *telling* them; you're asking them—or better yet, inviting them—to be still and stay with you. Touch them in a place that is comfortable for them.

Then find another place on their body they enjoy having caressed. Place your thumb on their body to anchor your hand. Move your other four fingers in a circle and a quarter from six o'clock around the clock back to 6:00 and keep going to nine o'clock. Take a second or two to complete the cycle, then stop, and allow their body to start to reset. Continue this pattern over different parts of their body so that their body "resets" itself without outside life force energy being introduced.

If you know massage, be careful not to use strong force. This isn't deep tissue massage or trigger point work! A pressure of a one or two on a scale of ten is best.

It seems to me that a body whose nervous system is running in the "peace" mode (parasympathetic autonomic system), even when not at optimal health, is more able to focus its remaining life force on keeping the body going—circulation, breathing, digesting, immunity, and normal elimination. In addition, your animal may more easily accept, rather than reject, outside interventions to help keep them going.

Time spent in the "stress" mode (sympathetic autonomic system) wastes the animal's remaining life force. This seems particularly important as we look for ways to help our animals maintain their life force and spend more time on the planet.

Put another way: Their life force could be considered the same as the money humans saved up for retirement. We are advised to spend our retirement money prudently, so it lasts as long as we live. TTouch may help our animals spend their life force "prudently" or with less effort because they're in the "peace" mode of their nervous system. Spending more time in the "peace" mode might lengthen their life. Who knows?

.   .   .

Why TTouch Works

There are dozens of studies on the effects and effectiveness of TTouch.[25] One of the positive effects of TTouch is that it softens the fascia, which is the thin casing of connective tissue that surrounds and holds every organ, blood vessel, bone, nerve fiber, and muscle in place. It's as sensitive as skin.

Want to bring comfort to your animal? If so, TTouch's effect on fascia might be useful. It also makes a connection to the limbic system in the brain, positively affecting emotions, which leads to less stress.

The Philosophy Behind TTouch

TTouch isn't pushed on our animals. Rather, we allow our animals to tell us whether they want to be worked on. We invite animals to accept the touch and allow them to walk away when they have enough. We look for collaboration with our animals and think in terms of guiding rather than controlling.

Isn't it wonderful to give our animals the power of consent? Much of their lives are dictated by what works for us and what behaviors we allow. When it comes to medical intervention, we make decisions for them because it's in their best interest. Not because they're saying, "Yippee! I love going to the veterinarian!" (Or most don't anyway; my dog Stella loves seeing all the lovely people at the vet's office.) The TTouch philosophy gives our animals choice in this interaction. It's healing for everyone.

ACUPUNCTURE

This section condenses a talk given on animal acupuncture by Dr. Jordan Kocen of the Veterinary Holistic Center in Springfield, Virginia. Acupuncture can help our animals regain mobility,[26] increase kidney function,[27] improve digestion, decrease pain, and decrease allergies.

As I write this section, my thirteen-year-old dog Stella is receiving acupuncture for mobility. What a useful tool for our animals! Acupuncture helps her get up and down our stairs again.

And, she enjoys longer walks more often than she did before the treatments.

What does Stella think about acupuncture? She isn't excited about her treatments, but once the very-thin needles are in, she's good with hanging out for a short while and getting a treat afterwards! In my experience, acupuncture's definitely worth looking into for a number of health issues.

Why Acupuncture Works

People familiar with Western medicine may find the Chinese medical theory of acupuncture affecting the flow of Chi (life force energy) difficult to believe or understand. Unfortunately, the theory only explained why acupuncture worked, not that it did or didn't work. Recent studies have supported the effectiveness of acupuncture for animals.

The Chinese mapped out results when a needle was put in a certain spot. For instance, they found, "If I put a needle here by the thumb, not only is it good for the thumb but it's good for a runny nose." They mapped acupuncture points for all sorts of ailments and symptoms.

From Western medical understanding, the body's main messaging system is electrical (the nervous system), and its secondary system is chemical (hormones and chemicals).

An acupuncture point is an area in the muscle layer under the skin that has a high concentration of nerve endings. When you put an acupuncture needle there, those nerves are stimulated. The initial response from the spinal cord is, "get that thing out of there." Blood flow increases. Tight muscles start to relax. The body releases anti-inflammatory chemicals and endorphins. White blood cells come and flush out toxins.

Usually, the acupuncture needles need to stay in place for about fifteen to twenty minutes, because not all nerves respond immediately. This gives the nervous system a better chance to do what it's going to do.

Generally, it takes three or four treatments to see if acupuncture is helping. If there's no improvement by the time six treatments are completed, then acupuncture probably won't work for your animal. Fortunately, that's rare.

Treatments are typically held once a week to every ten days for the first few visits. If there are improvements, the length of time between session is gradually extended. The longest interval that maintains and sustains them at that better level of function is optimal.

Where Animal Acupuncture is Effective

Animal acupuncture is great for stiffness, mobility, aches, and pains, as well as things related to the muscles, ligaments, and tendons. On the mobility front, Dr. Kocen shared that at least eighty percent of his patients showed improvements when using acupuncture.

As they age, many labs, golden retrievers, German shepherds, and giant breeds become slower and stiffer, their back-end lowers, they have trouble getting up, and they can't climb stairs, which can be signs of possible osteoarthritis.[28] Often, within just a few acupuncture treatments, these dogs are re-engaged with the family.

Interestingly, people notice that their dog or the cat's immune system improves after animal acupuncture. Others report lessened allergies and improved digestive systems. That's because many points used to support mobility are good for the liver, kidney, and other organs.

Let's not forget cats! Many aging cats are affected by kidney disease.[29] Acupuncture may help when they experience back tension/tightness. The tension may decrease nerve flow to their kidneys, which in turn diminishes the kidneys' function. Stimulating kidney acupuncture points improves communication between the kidneys and the central nervous system. This helps stimulate the kidneys to work better.

. . .

Potential Limitations

The longer a problem has been there, or the more physical problems animals have, the harder it'll be to help your animal, even with acupuncture. If they've lost nerve functions in key places, animal acupuncture will not work as well. If they have *some* nerve function, you'll usually see improvement.

Noticing Improvements

When deciding whether acupuncture is working, look for subtle improvements. Here are some examples Dr. Kocen has heard from people:

- This may sound funny, but she seems happier.
- There's a little more sparkle in their eyes.
- They're getting up and down easier.
- They want to go for walks; they're able to go for walks again.
- They're picking up their toys again.
- My neighbor said he sees the difference—I hadn't noticed it 'til then.

Needles! Ugh!

One of the biggest drawbacks that keep people away from acupuncture is their own memory of vaccinations or a blood draw—their own or their animals. Acupuncture needles, though, are different. Very thin, sterile, stainless-steel needles are used. They're so thin, you could put seven or eight of these needles inside a vaccine needle. That's how tiny these are. They're also short.

Most acupuncture points that are used for animals are along the back. With a little distraction—rubbing their ears or stroking their backs—animals barely notice the needles. The needles are not painful. Most clients are quite shocked at how well their animals do. The animals may look at you as if to say, "Why are we here? We could sit at home and do nothing for fifteen minutes!" Some even fall asleep!

Interactions with Medications

Acupuncture generally has no negative interactions with current medications, supplements, or treatments. That's mainly because each of these modalities work through different actions. Most veterinarians advise people to keep all medications and doses the same during initial treatment, so that an accurate assessment can be made as to the acupuncture's efficacy.

After the initial session and noted improvements, you can ask, "Which of these medications poses a (potential) problem?" Challenges could include digestive upsets or liver problems. Those are weened first. In many cases, the animals can at least decrease their medications, if not get off all pharmaceuticals.

ACUPRESSURE

Most of us aren't trained acupuncturists, but we can still use press or touch acupuncture points to assist our animals. That's acupressure. I wrote a blog post that focuses on dogs' nausea,[30] and you can use those same points on other animals. Tallgrass Animal Acupressure Resources' article, *Canine Anxiety and Stomach Chi*,[31] gives a great description of how to locate a few of the acupressure points for dog nausea.

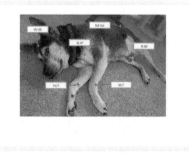

Below are some suggested acupressure points to help nausea:

- **Bai Hui**: *Very calming! It's that spot right in front of the tail that dogs love you to scratch!*
- **GV 20**:Calms the brain
- **Ki 27**:*Harmonizes the stomach*
- **Pe 7** and **Ht 7**: *Reduces anxiety and nausea*
- **St 36**: *Harmonizes the stomach*

Give these points a try and see how your animal reacts. To see if you're stimulating the right point, look for a relaxed response from your animal (sighing, putting head down, stretching, falling asleep, yawning, soft eyes). I noticed my dog Tibor enjoyed some points more than others (St 36 and Ki 27 were hits).

Animal Wellness' article, *Acupressure for your dog's stomach*,[32] reminds us to do the points on both sides of the body. For instance, points found on the back or front legs should be done on both the right and left legs. They're pretty much the same for other four-legged mammals.

The *Whole Dog Journal* article, *Acupressure Can Relieve Nausea*,[33] provides some great ideas for helping dogs with car nausea. They teach you two ways of manually working the acupressure points. These suggestions come from their article:

- An hour before the car ride, find a quiet place and perform the acupressure treatment.
- Keep car trips short at first after you do acupressure.
- If your dog looks uncomfortable, pull over and rest a bit. Redo the acupuncture treatments again before continuing.

Cat Nausea

For adventuresome types, an article from Tallgrass Animal Acupressure Resources, *Enhancing Feline Digestion with Acupressure*[34] shares good acupuncture points for cat digestion issues. I tried doing acupressure on St 36 for my cat, Mac. Let's just say he was not delighted. Read my blog, *When Your Cat Won't Eat*[35] for other ideas.

Anxiety When Visiting the Veterinarian More Often

Chances are your aging animal is spending more time at the veterinarian or being given medicines they love to take. So, decreasing their anxiety can be part of your strategy to keeping them (and you!) enjoying their senior years. Here are a few acupressure techniques you can use to calm them.

Bladder Meridian Sweep

You don't need to know any acupuncture points to do the Bladder Meridian Sweep technique,[36] which helps calm and ground your animal in any situation where they seem anxious. This can help when veterinary visits are increasing or you're giving your animals medication. My dogs allow me to practice this sweep, but my cats aren't impressed.

Additionally, I've seen the Bladder Meridian Sweep successfully used on horses. I imagine rabbits, rats, and guinea pigs who love to be touched will allow you to do this. I don't have experience with birds or reptiles, but I've seen birds stroked with a feather as the equivalent to massage, so that might work.

Here's how you do it:

- Ask your animal to stand up for you.
- Start at the top of their head between the ears and slide your hand down the right side of the spine, down the neck, and down the torso until you reach the tail.
- Continue to move your hand down the outside of their right leg to the outside of their right foot.
- Repeat from the top of the head along the left side of the neck, spine, and outside of the left leg to the outside of their left foot.

Congratulations! You just caressed them along the acupuncture Bladder Meridian!

I usually talk to my dogs about their anxiety while I do the sweep. I use positive words with a gentle voice. You can say sentences such as,

- "I take you to the veterinarian so you can continue to do what you love!"
- "You're safe, I will always be with you!"
- "I do everything I can because I love you. You can trust me. I want to help you feel better!"

These are just examples. Use the language that comes directly from your heart to theirs!

Relaxation Heart 1

Susan Tenney demonstrates another easy acupressure point to release tension in her video of the *Heart 1 acupressure point in the upper leg armpit crease.*[37]

COLD LASER TREATMENT

We already know that sunlight helps generate Vitamin D, which is essential for our body's health. Now we know that other frequencies of light can stimulate cell health as well. This is called low level or cold laser therapy. There's evidence that cold laser treatment helps with pain, inflammation and wound healing.[38] For science geeks, this ability to affect tissues is called cellular photo-biostimulation. According to an article from the American Animal Hospital Association,[39] laser therapy can also be used when medical treatment options are limited, such as animals with liver disease and are unable to take most medications. That's because it's a non-invasive modality.

My dog Stella received cold laser therapy while she was getting her acupuncture treatments to help with osteoarthritis. The veterinarian pointed the small hand-held device at her lower back as she sat on the floor with the acupuncture needles in place. She didn't react at all.

HERBAL MEDICINES

Herbal, or plant-based, medicine has always interested me. Before allopathic medicine (also called conventional medicine, mainstream medicine, orthodox medicine, and Western medicine) became the primary methodology of most doctors, healers used the power of plants to bring animals (human and otherwise) back to a healthier state.

The textbook, *The Principles and Practice of Phytotherapy: Modern Herbal Medicine*,[40] explains that human and our animals' bodies are designed to metabolize most plants. That's because we're related to plants on an evolutionary scale, and we've been ingesting them for tens of thousands of years.

Animals in the wild have used plants as medicine. For instance, in an article by Joel Shurkin, *Animals that Self-Medicate*,[41] we find:

Birds, bees, lizards, elephants, and chimpanzees all share a survival trait: They self-medicate. These animals eat things that make them feel better, or prevent disease, or kill parasites like flatworms, bacteria, and viruses, or just to aid in digestion. Even creatures with brains the size of pinheads somehow know to ingest certain plants or use them in unusual ways when they need them.

Some lizards are believed to respond to a bite by a venomous snake by eating a certain root to counter the venom. Red and green macaws, along with many animals, eat clay to aid digestion and kill bacteria.

Herbal medicine can be used for healing, boosting our animal's emotions, and pain relief.

WHAT HERBAL MEDICINE CAN TREAT

Metabolic Diseases: Liver and Kidney Changes

Herbal medicines can also help with metabolic diseases, such as liver and kidney changes, caused by exposure to toxins or other age-related diseases.

Chronic Problems: Skin, Digestion, and Respiration

Skin, digestion, and respiration problems are all longer-term inflammatory processes. Anti-inflammatory medicines may or may not control inflammation. If they do, they do have side effects. If you try to wean your animals off drugs, their problems may return because you simply were controlling the inflammation, not its cause.

Some herbal medicines can stimulate the body's immune system to decrease that inflammation. They may have fewer side effects than a pharmaceutical remedy.

Long-term Use is Okay

Herbs can be used for longer term. Older animals' immune systems get a bit weaker so there are immune tonics that enhance immune function.

Herbal Medicine Options

There are so many good options when you're considering herbal medicines, such as:

- Herbals medicines. May be dried or in liquid form.
- Flower essences (Bach Rescue Remedy).
- Traditional Chinese Medicine. Many herbal remedies are based in the Chinese medical system of maintaining the health of Chi, the animal's life force.

- Homeopathy. Not strictly plant based as this option may use minerals and animals.
- Essential oils. Fifty-to-seventy times more powerful than herbs.
- Hydrosols. The condensate water co-produced during steam or hydro-distillation of plants to make essential oils (some aromatherapists recommend these as a safer alternative to essential oils for smaller animals).

ESSENTIAL OILS

Although this section provides a wealth of information on essential oils, I am sure I have not covered everything. And there's always new research on the subject. So please do your own due diligence on using essential oils for your animals. Before I begin, I'd like to thank Debbie Tuttle, of Aspen Living, author of *Wealthy in the Woods,*[42] for her expertise in this area.

It's important to be cautious when using essential oils for animals. That's because information available on the web generally focuses on how essential oils may help humans. Essential oils that are safe for humans may not be safe for certain species. Do your homework!

What Are Essential Oils?

Here are the characteristics of essential oils:

- These are volatile liquids distilled from plants. Volatile means they evaporate at room temperature so keep the lid tight!
- They're *not* oily. If they feel oily, something has been added. This is only a problem if the producer claims they're 100% essential oils. You want to know what you're getting.
- They are created through steam distillation, cold expression (crushed and oils pulled out through centrifuge), or cold pressing.

- Cost based upon the difficulty of obtaining quality plant material.
- Documented use since 2500 BCE (China) and 1550 BCE (Egypt).

Essential Oils Might Kill Bacteria and Viruses

My interest in essential oils and bacteria/viruses piqued when I discovered that the Great Plague (Bubonic Plague) of Europe (1347-1353) killed somewhere between thirty to fifty percent of the European population in eight years. It has been reported that those most in contact with aromatics, such as perfumers, were less likely to contract the plague.

In the scientific research article, *Effect of Essential Oils on Pathogenic Bacteria*,[43] "Essential oils contain a wide variety of secondary metabolites that are capable of inhibiting or slowing the growth of bacteria, yeasts and moulds."

Another scientific research article, *Camphor—A Fumigant during the Black Death and a Coveted Fragrant Wood in Ancient Egypt and Babylon—A Review*,[44] includes, "Camphor exhibits several biological properties such as antimicrobial, antiviral and antitussive (relieves coughing) effects."

Watch for Adulteration of Essential Oils

The quality of essential oils is one of the key factors to ensure they're safe for your animal. Research to ensure non-herbal substances weren't added to your favorite brand of essential oil. Some manufacturers do add non-herbal or non-organic substances to their oils, and this can be harmful:

- Citrus peels in the essential oil. If they aren't organic, you're getting the pesticides with the oil.

- Base oil. Some companies may add fatty base oils to essential oils, which is not always labeled.
- Some may be diluted with synthetic fragrances oils. The problem is these synthetic fragrances have no therapeutic value and can cause skin irritations.
- Some oils may be diluted with less costly essential oils.
- Some manufacturers may dilute the oils with nature-identical chemicals. For instance, lavender may have synthetic linalyl acetate added to it. The synthetic isn't therapeutic.
- Some manufacturers may combine certain essential oils to mimic more expensive scents. Some have combined Black Pepper + Ylang Ylang to create Fake Carnation, which can be sold at the higher price as if it was the real thing

Why Do Some Manufacturers Use Synthetic Oils?

Plant qualities are based on the growing season they experience. My daughter is a farmer, and she taught me that crops of the same plant can differ depending on what weather Mother Nature provides that season.

But, synthetic oils are human created to be consistent. Man-made substances are usually cheap, and they are not usually plant based. Or, they may have some plant essences, but man-made substances have been added. That's so the manufacturer can add fragrance cheaply and consistently.

Use Your Discernment; Do Your Research

Read a number of sources as there are differing guidelines. It bears repeating that some plants and their essential oils are not suited for all species. So even after you have found a safe essential oil to use with your animal, still notice how your animals reacts to its application.

General Cautions

- Don't force essential oil use unless you have experience with your animal and it's an emergency.
- Skip "hot oils" for the most part (phenols), like cassia, cinnamon, clove, oregano, peppermint, thyme, wintergreen, and tea tree (melaleuca).
- Don't give essential oils orally to cats or smaller animals.

Check the Safety of Specific Oils in These Cases

- Epileptic/seizure-prone: Avoid basil, black pepper, camphor, eucalyptus, fennel, hyssop, sage, rosemary, and wintergreen.
- Bleeding disorders, difficulty clotting or being treated with an anticoagulant: Avoid topical application of oils such as birch, cassia, cinnamon, clove, fennel, oregano, and wintergreen.
- Pregnant or nursing animals: Avoid highly diluted hot oils cassia, cinnamon, clove, oregano, peppermint, thyme, wintergreen, and tea tree (melaleuca). Other oils to avoid include basil, cassia, cinnamon, clary sage, rosemary, thyme, wintergreen, and white fir.
- Puppies: For small breeds, wait until they're ten weeks old to use essential oils. For medium to large breeds, wait until they're eight weeks old.
- Kittens: Wait until kittens are at least ten weeks old before using essential oils.

Ways to Give Essential Oils to Animals
A general rule of thumb is to dilute the essential oil unless you're

letting your animal sniff the scent from your hand as a way to decide whether they want to try it.

For dogs and horses, you can put a couple of drops on your hand and warm them up so the smell is strong. Then let the dog or horse sniff your hand and observe their reaction. They may show interest, or even lick the oil, or move away. Unless it's an emergency, you might want to take your cue from their response as to whether to use the essential oil.

Aromatically

Let's assume you've already checked to see if the essential oil is safe for your animal. I recommend a water diffuser. This is a container of water in which you add a few drops essential oils. Once you plug it in and turn it on, the essential-oil infused water gets diffused into the air as a mist. The water is not heated.

Be sure your animals can get to fresh air if they need to. Open the window, or keep the door to the room with the diffuser open so they can move to another room for fresh air.

To test their reaction the first time, be sure to add no more than a few drops of essential oil in the diffuser. Diffuse no more than five-to-ten minutes and check their response.

Cats can take up to forty-eight hours to process diffused oils. So, for their safety, allow a couple of days in between diffusion sessions.

Topical Application of Essential Oils

We can handle undiluted essential oils, but don't expect your animals to tolerate them like you do. Essential oils can be diluted by adding them to carrier oils like olive oil or coconut oil.

Remember, most animals' sense of smell is much better than humans. Even birds have a sense of smell—the latest research overturns a long-held belief that birds don't have the ability or need to smell. You probably won't endear yourself to your animals by applying undiluted pungent essential oils to their bodies where they can't get away from the smell. Instead, use essential oils which are diluted with a carrier oil or water.

1. Pet along the spine. I find my dogs accept this.
2. Ear tipping. Apply the diluted oil to the tips of an animals' ears. Some animals tolerate this, but many do not. Avoid using this type of application with long-eared dogs as they may shake their head and get the oil in their eyes accidentally.
3. Apply to paws. This is not always very well tolerated in small animals. Be sure to get it on the skin between the paw pads. This is a fairly sensitive area, so be sure to use diluted oils.
4. Water misting. This is great for birds: add a drop of oil to several ounces of water, shake, and spritz on the animal. This is also helpful for large animals if you want to cover a larger area, or they don't tolerate regular handling.
5. Large animals. You can put the essential oil where the hoof meets the skin, or the coronet band. This is very helpful when treating foot conditions or lameness issues in horses.
6. Add to other topical products such as shampoo or coconut oil.
7. Indirect application. Apply to bedding or an area your animal frequently comes into contact with. Remember their keen sense of smell means a little goes a long way.

Internal Application of Essential Oils

Using essential oils internally has a limited application. It's primarily offered as an option for dogs and horses. Always check with a holistic veterinarian *before* you let your animal ingest essential oils. Often topical application will work just as well as internal application.

1. In a capsule. One drop per capsule, then top off the rest with an animal-safe carrier oil like olive oil or coconut oil.
2. In food. People usually recommend adding essential oils to wet food mixed either with a carrier oil or directly into the wet food.
3. In drinking water. The bowl must be glass, ceramic, or stainless steel, and the essential oil must be very diluted. Make sure the water is high quality.

Warning: Topical Application Can Equal Internal Application

Remember for animals who groom themselves frequently, such as cats, birds, dogs, rabbits, and chinchillas, topical application also means internal application. If this happens and the oil was applied topically, dilute it by applying a vegetable oil, such as fractionated coconut oil, directly over the area.

Warning Signs of Bad Reaction to Essential Oils

Here are general warning signs of a potentially negative reaction to essential oil usage. If you see these signs, get medical advice as soon as possible:

- Dizziness.
- Lack of appetite.
- Vomiting.
- Incoordination or lack of balance.
- Difficulty breathing.
- Fragrance/scent on their coat, skin or breath after ingestion.
- Drooling.
- Lethargy or weakness.

Essential Oils and Cats

Cats lack an enzyme in their liver that is important in the metabolism of many types of things. This makes cats susceptible to *all* kinds of toxicity, including certain plants, NSAIDS (like aspirin, ibuprofen and Tylenol), chocolate, caffeine (methylxanthines), lead, zinc, and many pesticides.

Do not apply (topically or internally) these essential oils to your cats: basil, birch, cinnamon, clove, fennel, melaleuca, nutmeg, oregano, peppermint, thyme, rosemary, spearmint, and wintergreen. Also, be cautious using bergamot, dill, pine oil, and citrus like grapefruit, lemon, lime, orange, tangerine.

Essential Oils and Small Mammals: Hindgut Fermenters

Hindgut fermenters, such as rabbits, guinea pigs, sugar gliders, chinchillas, and hamsters, have a delicate digestive flora. Be careful with essential oils that have strong anti-bacterial properties such as cinnamon, cassia, and oregano. You don't want to inadvertently disrupt digestion.

Check into the use of hydrosols instead of essential oils.

Essential Oils and Birds

Water-based diffusion is likely the best way to introduce essential oils for most birds, unless they are in a very large area.

Misting using a mixture of water and the essential oil is another way to deliver essential oils to birds. Birds often enjoy being misted with water for bathing. When essential oils are added to this "ritual," we find birds enjoy it even more. Routine exposure to essential oils may keep them healthy, and aid in hormonal issues, skin conditions, feather picking, and emotional concerns.

Essential Oils and Horses

According to my research, oils and oil blends that work for dogs also seem to work for horses. Horses have powerful noses, so don't increase the percent of essential oil in carrier oils or blends. Never use undiluted essential oils on the skin.

Everyday Essentials by Plant Therapy[45] suggests you allow your horse to smell a diluted (one to two percent) essential oil before you use it on them. Rub it on your palms to allow your horse to smell it. Do they respond positively, negatively, or indifferently? If you see a happy response, continue a few more days. Then, move on to diffusion and topical inhalation.

Hydrosols

As hydrosols are the condensed water co-produced during steam or hydro-distillation of plants to make essential oils, some aromatherapists recommend these as a safer alternative to essential oils for smaller animals, including birds.

CANNABIS OR CBD (CANNABIDIOL)

More U.S. states and countries outside the U.S. have legalized cannabis. Nevertheless, at this time, it's still on Schedule 1 List as a "drug" under the U.S. Controlled Substance Act. Even in those U.S. states where cannabis is legal for humans, it may still be illegal for veterinarians to prescribe. That's why you'll find CBD more available since it is generally made from hemp rather than cannabis (marijuana).

According to the book, *Cannabis for Canines* by Beverly A. Potter, Ph.D.:

The American Holistic Veterinary Medical Association
(AHVMA) is the first veterinary organization to officially
encourage research in the use of cannabis for animals. They
said, 'There is a growing body of veterinary evidence that
cannabis can reduce pain and nausea in chronically ill or
suffering animals, often without the fulling effects of narcotics.

This herb may be able to improve the quality of life for many patients, even in the face of life-threatening illnesses.'...The Aussies took the lead when in February 2016, Australia legalized medicinal cannabis at its federal level.

My human family members have used specific cannabis strains for chronic pain, nausea, and anxiety. These strains emphasize the medical properties and minimize the "getting high" properties.

Do your own research, but here's how cannabis or CBD oil may help your animal's quality of life (Note: this is NOT medical advice; I'm not a veterinarian):

- Digestive upsets.
- Anxiety and phobias. Some dog guardians were able to replace Prozac and Paxil with CBD oils.
- Arthritis and joint stiffness.
- Skin hot spots.
- Malaise and lethargy.
- Epilepsy and seizures.
- Heart and circulatory issues.
- Pain and inflammation.

My mistake with CBD use was when I gave Stella too much.[46] My husband thought she was on her way out because she was so lethargic on her walks. I figured out the issue and corrected the dosage, and she's interested in walking again.

REHAB

In addition to chiropractic and acupuncture for animals, you might consider a rehab specialist (fun fact: rehab specialists are called physical therapists when working with humans). Many middle-aged and older dogs benefit from rehab specialists just as middle-aged and older people benefit from physical therapy. Rehab focuses on exercises to stretch and strengthen core muscles.

Rehab specialists will show you exercises and offer homework to do with your animal (probably a dog or horse). These are mostly supportive exercises. You can also use rehab post-operatively to get back to fully functional.

Underwater Treadmill

When I first heard the term "underwater treadmill," I imagined one of my dogs using a snorkel as they walked underwater on the treadmill. Thankfully, no snorkels needed! The treadmill is under water, which relieves the pressure of walking for the animal. It's similar to humans doing aqua aerobics when they're having a hard time doing the exercises in a regular setting.

As you can guess, dogs with mobility issues can use an underwater treadmill. Typically, a rehab specialist directs the therapy, and the result is two-fold: conditioning and strengthening. While you *can* walk them "out of water" for similar results, you'll have to walk a long time, find hills, and boost their strength.

Imagine a plexiglass chamber, eight-feet long and three-feet wide. Dogs walk inside, the rehab specialist turns on the water, which fills up from the bottom. Once the water has reached a certain level, the treadmill is turned on. When the dog walks, they're pushing against the water.

Some dogs can't walk far because they're overweight, older, and weaker. The height of the water in the underwater treadmill pool is adjusted to provide a little bit of buoyancy, so it takes some of the weight off their joints. When the treadmill is activated, they still have to walk, but their joints don't bear all the weight.

After a dog's knee surgery, your surgeon may recommend you get your dog into rehab to stretch their muscles and get them walking again. By using water treadmill therapy, their knees aren't negatively impacted due to the resistance provided by the water.

HOMEOPATHY

Homeopathy is based on the concepts of "less is more" and "like cures like." It uses minute amounts of natural substances to jumpstart the body's healing process. Homeopathic treatments come in tiny pellets that are taken orally (they taste like small sugar cubes). These can be dissolved in water as well. The medicine may also come as a liquid or a powder.

David Sollars wrote, "Homeopathy gained its initial popularity in Europe and the United States during the 1800s because of its successful nontoxic treatment of infectious epidemics that savaged both continents. During that time, medical cures were often as dangerous as the diseases."[47]

It's best to visit a homeopathic certified veterinarian when choosing the homeopathic route for chronic symptoms. They will ask questions about your animal's personality and lifestyle as well as their symptoms. This way, they can create just the right medicine for your animal. Typically, you should give the medicine at least an hour before or after your animal eats.

If you use over-the-counter remedies, research to ensure there are no problems with the manufacturer or product. I use a few over-the-counter homeopathic remedies for myself but have visited a homeopathic veterinarian for my animals.

CRYSTALS

I'd like to thank Dahlia of Crystal Cognizance in Alexandria, Virginia, for sharing information about crystals with us during an interview in the spring of 2021.[48]

Crystals bring a perfect structure and vibration to healing. Think of living animals as mushy, gushy, malleable, and easily changed beings. Crystals, however, are not that way. They are fixed and hard to influence. It takes a great deal of pressure, atmospheric changes, or heat to alter a crystalline structure. Living animals have a crystalline structure within as well. Crystals bring a literal grounding element to our healing needs.

How Do Crystals Work?

When you hold a still and solid object, a little bit of you comes back to yourself. This is known as grounding. As you work with the vibration of the stone, it begins to influence and alter you in interesting ways.

If you understand the purpose of a crystal, your subconscious mind says, "Oh right. This helps me with that." So now your subconscious mind is bringing you back to yourself (grounding you) even further. And, if you were given that particular crystal with the intention of love from another person, that love brings you back to yourself a little bit more. This feels particularly true when we pick crystals for our animals!

This subtle and incremental change can occur over a fifteen-to-twenty-minute period with people. With animals, it's much faster, which is what makes crystals amazing.

Use Crystals to Work on Yourself and Your Animals

It is important to treat both you and your animals because emotions between us can be entangled. Our animal partners are empaths. Empaths are capable of absorbing energy, then changing it, healing it, resolving it, and sending it back out. That's what's supposed to happen, but empathic animals may stop at the absorption process. They may pick up and hold what we're feeling. That's when they may have problems. This is why you may see animals deteriorate quickly in households in extreme turmoil.

If you have an animal with a chronic condition, it's important to pause and ask questions. What's going on with the people in the house? Is your house on a lay line, or near power lines, or affected by something environmental? Remember, animals are more sensitive to the environment than we are at first glance.

Animals have their own issues, and they're also dealing with their own karma (Note: karma is just energy that needs to be finished). They are working through their own soul's lessons. Ask yourself, "Are there crystals I could use to support their work?"

Crystals for Anxiety, Grounding, and Communicating

Anxiety is the fear of what's to come. It is takes us out of the present moment. Also, anxiety is not knowing what's going on around you. Crystals can help facilitate a heart connection of, "Ah, I can feel that all is well with my family."

Ask yourself, "Where is this anxiety coming from?" The answer is not the same for everybody. Anxiety is simply a symptom and can take many forms, such as:

- Am I being taken away from somebody I love? (Maybe they're feeling this if they're required to be hospitalized for a longer period of time.)
- You changed the routine in the house. What's going on? (More visits to the veterinarian than in the past could create this feeling.)
- My person is uncomfortable and there's nothing I can do to alleviate that. (They might be feeling our own sadness and fear about their declining health or mental abilities.)

For separation anxiety, the crystals to reach for include mangano calcite, rose quartz, amethyst, or fluorite. Mangano calcite is a beautiful and very soothing stone. It helps dissolve conflict. It taps into unconditional love in a way that is deeper than rose quartz. And, it facilitates connection and understanding.

Black and red grounding stones like red jasper, obsidian, jet, tourmaline, and hematite will also help with anxiety. Use love, and you will have an ability to have a beautiful impact on your animals, especially when it comes to separation anxiety

If you have challenges with your animal and want to understand what's going on, hold mangano calcite in your hand, and bring it close to your animal. Hold the crystal near them and say, "I'm here for you." You may gain an understanding of what your animal is going through, without projecting your issues on them.

Amethyst's perfect crystalline structure carries the vibration of iron. Iron is grounding. It's purifying and will bring you and your animal right back into your center.

Aquamarine, amazonite, petilite, and pink tourmaline are beautiful communication stones. These stones take us back to that heart healing place—and telepathy is heart-based, not a third-eye practice. Our animals are so receptive to communication through the heart.

Unsafe Crystals

Malachite and hematite are dangerous for animals. There are also other dangerous crystals.[49] Determine whether the crystal you're using is safe. If it's toxic, don't allow your animals to munch on or swallow it.

Crystal Healing for Our Animals

One way to give our animals crystal healing is to place the stones on their bodies. Of course, you should stay with them and monitor them at all times if you choose to do this.

You probably don't want your animals to wear crystals. If they fall off, your animals might eat or gnaw on them. That's because they love the crystal's energy. Plus, other animals might be exposed through play.

You can also create a crystal elixir for your animal. A crystal elixir is water that has absorbed the energy of the crystal. Then it's either imbibed by your animal or sprayed on them, so they receive the energetic properties of the crystal.

There are two ways to create the elixir depending on whether the crystal is safe or toxic. If the crystal is safe, you can set the stone directly in the water, so the water receives the energy from the stone.

If you know it's toxic for human/animal consumption or you're not sure whether it's safe, put the crystal in a glass. Then place the glass in the water so there's no direct contact between the crystal and the water. Glass is a great medium to protect the water from the physical properties of the crystal but still allow the crystal's energetic properties to permeate the water.

Let it charge for six to twelve hours. Sunlight will also help the crystal charge the water. After at least six hours, remove the crystals. Let your animal drink the water or spray them with the crystal elixir.

8

ENERGY HEALING
AND MEDICAL INTUITION

> The thoughts we think, the prayers we offer, the good
> we do in this world live on, influencing and affecting not
> only our souls after death, but also the world we leave
> behind. In other words, nothing ever dies.

— ROBERT J. GRANT, *THE PLACE WE CALL HOME*

I'D LIKE to give you a clearer idea on how energy healing and medical intuition can be useful for helping you navigate your animal's last chapter of life.

In its simplest form, energy healing harnesses the highest vibration or highest energy, which is love. This love can be personal based on our relationship with our animal. It must also be spiritual, which is unselfish compassion and love focusing on another being's highest good. It's the essence of Creator's love for all Creation.

In most of my sessions that deal with physical issues, I offer medical intuition and energy healing as well as animal communication. It's a great combination. We find out how the animal is feeling physically and emotionally and get a feel for what lane of the Beltway of Life they're driving in most of the time. Then I am guided to offer an energy healing that feels most beneficial for the animal.

In many cases, there's some healing for their human, too. This healing is needed because humans accompany animals on their drive, helping them navigate the beltway, changing lanes when necessary, even helping them pick their exit. It's not easy. Energy healing can help us find the strength to keep going.

WESTERN SCIENCE AND MEDICINE

Before we go further, let's look at Western medicine to understand more clearly how Energy Healing is different.

When you visit your veterinarian, you receive science-based information on your animal's condition that has its foundation in Classical or Newtonian Physics. It's real and it's useful.

We're comfortable with Classical/Newtonian Physics because we live it every day. The old story about how Sir Isaac Newton "discovered" gravity is a fun example. He's sitting under an apple tree when an apple drops and hits him on the head. Sir Isaac says, "Oww!" as he discovers *and* curses gravity. The story's a bit of a myth, but a good one.

Classical Physics works to predict the outcome when one physical object interacts with another physical object. When we figure out the rules (like the Law of Gravity), we can accurately predict the results and figure out ways to improve those results for a better outcome. Most of the beneficial aspects of Western medicine are based on this model of how the physical world works.

ENERGY HEALING

When you enter the realm of Energy Healing, you've stepped from the world of Classical Physics to Quantum Physics. Quantum Physics studies particles smaller than atoms to see how they act, and scientists discovered that they don't follow the rules of Classical Physics.

These subatomic particles don't seem to be constrained by distance or time; everything that exists is a wave and a particle at the same time so it's both energetic and physical. And, non-physical realms, such as emotions, memories and thoughts, actually do affect the physical world on the Quantum Physics level. It's like two realities are operating at the same time.

This means I don't have to be in the room with your animal to do effective energy healing (although it is lovely when I can be)! When I do remote healing, sometimes people will ask me if their animal needs to be in the room or if they should put their phone on speaker so their animal can hear me. The answer is no. The Internet and phone are strictly for you and me, so we can communicate in the Classical Physics World. Your animal and I are communicating, and they're receiving a healing just fine in the Quantum Physics World.

DO-IT-YOURSELF SIMPLE ANIMAL ENERGY HEALING

Here are a few guidelines and modalities you can use to connect and send healing to your own animals.

1. Set your intention to help your animal heal.
2. The body has an intelligence, even a consciousness of its own. How else could it maintain breath, digestion, and posture, without us having to constantly direct it to do so? I believe the body prioritizes its issues, and will choose to heal or improve the issue that it feels is the top priority. Accept that whatever is most important is being worked on.
3. There will always be results, but they may be subtle or different than what we expected (see above). Healing can be physical, spiritual, emotional, or mental.
4. Do the Energy Healing that works for you. There are thousands of modalities for healing, and different personalities will be attracted to different modalities. If it works and it's healthy for your animal, celebrate it!

LESS IS MORE WITH ENERGY HEALING

In my experience, "less is more" when it comes to energy healing with animals. Pushing energy on to an animal is not as healing as offering gentle energy. Generally, people can accept stronger energy than animals. I don't think that's a compliment, though. For humans, energy seems to have to push through more layers of upsetting thoughts and emotions to get to a healing vibration than is required for an animal's healing.

Since animals create fewer barriers to healing than humans, a little healing can go a long way. Think of strong energy as a hailstorm pelting your body with hard chunks of ice. Now imagine gentle energy as a very light, warm misty rain you might experience in Hawaii. Stop for a moment and feel the difference in these energies. Your body and your energy field tighten up to protect in the first example. Conversely, you turn toward the rain and bask in the soft cleansing it brings your body and soul.

Finally, be mindful of when your animal tells you they've had enough. Usually, they'll move away or leave the room. Or, they'll give you the "stink eye" (enough already!). Don't take it personally or think you've done something wrong. I say, "Okay, then, guess we're done here. Let me know when you're up for more."

Sometimes after I say that they come back in the room and sit back next to me as if to say, "Oh, it's my choice? Well, then, I'll have some more thank you."

EMPATHY IS A GOOD VIBRATION

I've noticed that our bodies are always trying to do their best to keep us on the planet. They manage imbalances, pulling resources from one area to help another area, to keep the body going (until they can't anymore). I have a lot of empathy and respect for the body. No matter what's going on, it's doing the best it can under the circumstances. So, I bring forward empathy for their body's willingness to keep on keeping on. Especially as our animals decline, take time to thank both them *and* their bodies for doing what it takes to stay on the planet. That's a healing vibration in itself.

And I have a bit more empathy for some of the living beings like bacteria and viruses who are "doing their thing" to stay alive. Some of those I've connected with aren't personally attacking the body out of malice. Rather, they're searching for a home or sustenance. A good analogy might be squirrels in the attic. They didn't move into your attic to ruin your house; even though if they stay long enough, their urine may cause the ceiling to cave in (this happened to a neighbor). From the squirrel's point of view, they found a safe place for their family that's out of the weather with no predators. Here's a blog about my work with my mother-in-law's Shingles virus.

Before 2015, scientists did not think viruses were alive. Recently, they decided they were living organisms. So, I was finally able to call this an animal communication story.

I was working with my mother-in-law, Pat, practicing remote energy healing. We'd get on the phone three times a week and I'd work on whatever ailed her. I really enjoyed our time together. One time I asked, "What's going on?" She had shingles, which can feel like your skin is on fire. Pat was pretty uncomfortable.

I enlisted Pat's antibodies with the intention of going to war to clear out the virus. I gave it my all, trying to blast the virus out. In our next chat, I asked how she was feeling.

"Worst night of my life!" she exclaimed.

Well, that was a shock and certainly not the outcome I anticipated. I tried a different approach. I imagined that I was hosting an ice cream social outside—lots of flavors of ice cream, a picnic table, and trees for shade. I invited the virus and the antibodies to my party.

I told the virus, "Obviously, you aren't going anywhere! But consider that Pat's body is your home. The longer she is comfortable, the longer you have a home. How about going dormant and just enjoying what you have?" I asked the antibodies to call off their "five-alarm fire" response, pull back and allow the virus to go quiet.

Pat's next report was that she had gotten her first good night's sleep since the outbreak. There were no more shingles episodes the rest of her time on earth.

Nowadays, I will sometimes explain to the organism that their time is up. They need to leave the body or transform themselves into an organism that helps their host stay well. It's not a far-fetched request – our gut microbiome has 300-500 bacteria to help us digest our food. Why not one more useful bacterium?

THE ENERGETIC GREEN SMOOTHIE^{SM}

Here's a technique that connects you to your animals and allows you to send love to them. I originally created the Energetic Green Smoothie for my human family. My second husband, Charlie—never married, no kids—married me just as my two kids were on the brink of their teens. We'd lost their father (my first husband) Winston, unexpectedly about three years earlier. I bet you can imagine how greatly I desired to open everyone's heart to each other—so many emotions and new relationships. The Energetic Green Smoothie came in handy.

I soon realized this energy healing technique was a natural for families with animals. It connects and opens everyone's hearts. Communications and connections become infused with the energy of love. New arrivals feel part of the tribe. Current family members get a chance to connect with new arrivals through heart energy. And, it helps members in conflict consider the pluses of an improved relationship. This technique alone can strengthen your intuitive communication channel with your animals!

How to do the Energetic Green Smoothie

Use the heart chakra[50] energy to connect everyone's hearts. This chakra is green and—no surprise—carries the vibration of personal love for others and being loved by others. If you'd like to see how to do the Energetic Green Smoothie, you can watch this video on my YouTube channel.[51]

Ready? Picture yourself and your family in a circle. Remember, family includes your animals as well as your humans. If it's just the two of you, face each other in your mind's eye.

See a green, glowing light come out of your heart to touch the heart of the soul/being on your left. Then watch it move from their heart to the next being's heart, and the next—until the light returns to your heart.

Feel the love you have for this group and send it into the green light. Imagine the light moving gently around the circle back to you. Keep it moving as you imagine each heart is "melting with love."

You can do this any time with just your animal who is declining. You might "say" something to them in your mind, such as:

- I will always be there for you, no matter what.
- I know you [threw up/ eliminated on the carpet] because you're not feeling well. Don't worry, I'm not mad.
- I will take you for medical care, so you'll feel better and stay with us longer.
- I give you that funny tasting stuff/eyedrops, etc., because I want to help you stay well.
- I am so grateful you're still with us!

The Green Smoothie comes in handy when you take your animals to the veterinarian. For example, if you take them in for surgical procedure, explain what will happen, including their recovery. Remind them as each stage happens: going in for surgery, picking them up, and restrictions (how long and why). If your animals need to stay at the veterinarian for treatment, explain that they might be there overnight (or however long it will be).

You can also use it to connect with other family animals to explain what's happening to their friend, which helps relieve everyone's stress a bit. Think about using this technique when humans are ill, too. Even bad news is better than wondering why Harry's going to the veterinarian so often or why Mom's spending a lot of time in bed.

And give your animals a chance to say goodbye. Tell them they'll always be in each other's hearts. You may have to bring them together after one passed away so they *know* it's okay. Trust that if you explain what's going on, they'll pick up on it on some level. Reassure when you can but *always* tell the truth.

Once you've done the Energetic Green Smoothie a few times, you'll find that it's easy to do and also easy to remember. Each time you connect, you're sending loving Energy Healing along with any communication. Just set your intention to send love to connect their hearts, seeing and feeling the love and the color. Who doesn't love an easy energy communication/healing technique?

QUANTUM-TOUCH®

My friend, Psychic Bob Hickman, once told me during a reading, "I don't know what Quantum-Touch is, but you should check it out!"

He was right. It's s a great energy healing modality. Already a Reiki Master, I bought Richard Gordon's book, *Quantum-Touch: The Power to Heal,*[52] and started practicing the exercises. Because it was easy to understand and learn, I became a certified Quantum-Touch® practitioner.

In my experience with Quantum-Touch, body pain levels decreased faster, and positive physical changes occurred more often or quicker than simply using Reiki.

Gordon's step-by-step explanation on how to move energy through your body and help others heal was extraordinary.

You use a "breathe and sweep" technique that moves energy into your body as you breathe in and then out your arms as you breath out. In time, many people feel the energy move.

And, his explanation of resonance and entrainment is one of the best explanations of how energetic healing happens. Gordon shared:

There truly is a mystery and a wonder in the seemingly simple function of resonance. From the galaxies to the subatomic, all people and particles dance to its power…when two systems are oscillating at different frequencies, this is an impelling force called resonance that causes the two to transfer energy from one to another.

[E]ntrainment [is] a phenomenon that allows two similarly tuned systems to align their movement and energy so that they match in rhythm and phase…when working with Quantum-Touch, the practitioner holds the highest vibration they can, which becomes the dominant frequency…. All they are doing is providing the resonant energy to allow others to heal themselves.

Learn and practice these techniques if they call to you. Both have brought me and my animals' comfort and healing.

TRY ENERGY HEALING

Before you start the energy healing session, you might have to cry first to release the sadness you hold, knowing that your animal is declining. Allow your body to use the tears to release any pent-up sadness. Releasing your tears is better than holding it in because unacknowledged sadness might get in the way of pure energetic healing. Here are the steps to follow:

1. If you were a dog, I'd ask you to shake it off! Since you're not, do whatever works to move to the next step. I stare at

clouds, trees, and birds, and feel gratitude for their presence.

2. Next, feel the love you have for your animal. If you have ethereal beings you trust, ask them to assist you. Ask them to create a sacred space for you and your animal, a place where only love and light exists.

3. Set your intention to bring Creator's healing into your animal in whatever way is most beneficial for your animal. You can include intentions of physical healing and comfort. Maybe you want them to know that whatever you're doing for them is done for their highest physical good to help them feel better.

4. If it feels right, touch them and imagine the energy of your love enmeshed with your intentions traveling into their body. If you can't touch them, imagine the energy is traveling from your heart, hands, and head into their body. Remember, less is more; keep it gentle.

5. If it's easy for you, imagine a color going into them. If that's not easy, imagine an energy that relaxes them through and through. Notice if they sigh or yawn or settle into a super comfortable position. Imagine their body and Higher Self saying, "Oh, yummy, thanks, this is good stuff. I know just what to do with it." Imagine your animal feeling cozy and loved.

Congratulations! You're doing it! Continue to use your imagination as you ask for guidance on what will be best for your animal. Doing this will also calm you and that alone is healing for your animal. Your energy level can be healing, too. Being in a calm state whenever you can manage it will help your animal maintain their life force.

MEDICAL INTUITION: GRADUATE LEVEL ENERGY HEALING

One of the basic tenets of Energy Healing is that negative energy manifests first in our energetic body, which is both in and around our physical body. Negative energy can include negative thoughts, memories, and emotions from experiences, judgements, and beliefs. These energies weaken the energetic body over time. If they continue over years, they finally manifest in the physical body as illness and disease.

My Medical Intuition training with Tina Zion offered very focused procedures to clear negative energies associated with illnesses and disease (as well as behavioral issues). Even though Tina's procedures were designed for humans, I tailored many of them for animals as well.

Just like humans, animals' energy fields can become weakened from negative energies into their energy field. This seems to come from harsh experiences their mothers experienced or harsh experiences they personally endured. These energies can become dark, sluggish and dense energy. (Healthy energy is light, sometimes sparkly and moves easily.)

With Tina's training, I now work with animals to clear specific, dense energy from the animals' bodies. First, I invite Sacred Divine Beings who specialize in medical intuition to assist me in "seeing" the energy in and around the animal's body. Then I ask to be shown the cause for that dense energy. After sharing that with the person, we ask Sacred Divine Beings who are Master Healers to extract these energies from the animal's life force body and replace them with divine love in a way that is perfect for their healing.

After, we send the heavy energies to what I call the Ethereal Love Center to be transmuted into Love and Light. That way, they don't float around waiting for someone else to hang out with. I say a prayer that this energy might remember what it's like to find joy in the vibration of love.

It's comforting to share these healing modalities with people whose animals have grave illnesses and diseases. It's such a comfort to know that their animals will not have to carry this energy with them when they transition. And, in one case, the healing brought joy back into the life of a dog that we thought was ready to transition from cancer in the next forty-eight hours. That joy extended her life. Joy is always a blessing.

9

GETTING READY
FOR THE TRANSITION

> We are mortals all, human and nonhuman, bound in one
> fellowship of love and travail. No one escapes the fate of
> death. But we can, with caring, make our good-byes less
> tormented. If we broaden the circle of our compassion,
> life can be less cruel.
>
> — GARY KOWALSKI, *THE SOULS OF ANIMALS*

AT SOME POINT, the transition discussion starts happening for real. There will be ups and downs, but the transition thoughts are hard to ignore now. I know I cannot take away the grief of losing someone you love, human or not. At least with animals, you have the ability to reflect on how you will let them go. At least, in most cases, you have that ability—a gift and a burden at the same time.

MAKE A PLAN

You can include your own limitations in your plan. Not all of us are Florence Nightingale, with the ability and stamina to nurse a sick animal until they expire on their own. As animals age, we face new challenges. We might want to spare them and ourselves the final phase if it's going to be slow and painful.

In a National Public Radio (NPR) interview, veterinary behaviorist Nicholas Dodman, former head of the Animal Behavior department at Tufts Cummings School of Veterinary Medicine, pointed out that animals may decline physically, become incontinent, or act as if they're becoming senile.[53]

One question that arises during this time is, "Can we take care of an ailing animal the way they deserve?" And as we age, we may become less able to take care of an ailing animal. There's a great article in the Resources section of this book that provides ideas if you realize you can't take care of your animal like you want to.

Truthfully, we may have monetary limitations as well. If you've reached a monetary limit with your animal, check to see if a local charity might help you pay for your animal's care. There are a lot more of these than I imagined!

Another question to consider is, "Is your animal still enjoying life?" Maybe you're unable to keep them comfortable anymore or keeping them comfortable means they're groggy all the time and unable to interact with life. Assess which lane of the Beltway of Life they're on. Are they at the exit and can't quite make it off, stuck in an uncomfortable place?

Give yourself a permission slip that reads, "You're allowed to do what's best for everyone." When you think it might be the end, set your intention to do what's best for your family, which includes your animal. See your veterinarian for advice on the symptoms. Consider what you have to do to be ready to release them to the afterlife.

ALL BELOVED ANIMALS DESERVE CARE

Sometimes people think only certain animals (dogs, cats, horses) are worth helping through transition. But Erin Patricia Doherty's experience with her flock of budgies[54] asks us to rethink this prejudice.

A graduate of my UConnect Animal Communication class and a Reiki Master healer, Erin shared how mindfully navigating her birds' transition was important for them, their flock mates, and Erin. Here are some highlights of her wisdom in helping as her birds transitioned:

Mister Henry and Nickole. Photo Credit: Erin Patricia Doherty.

Bringing good energy around the birds was key, especially when they prepared to transition. They needed to know it was okay to leave their bodies when life got to be too much of a struggle. For this to happen, they had to be unencumbered by people's sorrow or anxiety.

It was important to be fully present and tune into their pain levels to maximize their comfort levels. Noticing what comforted each bird was key. Some wanted to be on their perch as long as they could. Others wanted to cuddle with Erin. A good practice is to notice what comforts your animal who's declining.

Even with birds, you may be able to pick up their readiness to transition. As Erin received more bad news from her veterinarian about Nickole, she was certain Nickole was going to transition. And shortly thereafter, euthanasia became necessary. Nickole's mate, Mister Henry, provided comfort before Nickole drew her last breaths in Erin's hands.

Bringing negative energy, such as pity, to sick, injured, or dying animals was not helpful. Try keeping the sad energy to yourself. Instead, send good healing or comforting energy from a place of love and compassion.

Although he was there when Nickole passed, Mister Henry forgot Nickole was really gone. He kept making the flock distance call to Nickole, waiting for her response. It was heartbreaking. From that experience, we know birds grieve after they've lost a mate, just like many mammals grieve.

After they transition, forgiveness is so important. We're not required to beat ourselves up for not knowing something that could have either saved a bird or increased their quality of life.

As you read Erin's experience with her birds, I would love you to help whatever animal you love to transition No matter what species they are. Don't be embarrassed to connect. Express your love, even if no one else understands your affection for your non-dog/cat/horse!

CREATE A BEAUTIFUL ENDING

Then think how you can create an ending that although sad, gives you comfort when you think of that day. Tell them you're ready to let them go and ask them if they have any desires. Think about what they really love and then decide:

- Where and how will it happen?
- Who should be there?
- What do you need to say to your animal before they pass?
- How will you celebrate or remember their life after they have passed?

As we all do, I have mixed memories of my animals' last day on earth. Some memories are touching, some are more difficult. All those memories leave me with a sense of loss. I also feel gratitude for the time those wonderful animals spent with me.

Another graduate of my UConnect animal communication class, Nancy Senger, and I worked together to help her dog April get ready for her last day. This picture includes Nancy, April (brindle greyhound), and Lucy (black greyhound), Nancy's other dog.

Nancy hugs April and Lucy. Photo credit: Nancy S.

After April's passing, Nancy sent me a lovely email sharing her experiences leading to April's last day on earth. When I asked Nancy if I could share her email with you, she responded, "Of course! My feelings are so deep for April—just as so many of us feel for our animals. Maybe it can help others deal with their wonderful animal's passing. It may help your readers to realize that it doesn't mean they are gone—they will remain forever in our hearts. They can always bring a smile to your face as you relive and remember their precious moments! I had to share this story because it helps me release my sadness."

Nancy shares the story of April's last day:

On Wednesday, April's eyes were bright and shiny. I thought I would have her a bit longer. Not so. On Thursday, April let me know she could no longer stand the pain. Truly, her eyes were a window to her soul!

The weather was rainy and supposed to be bad until Saturday. Knowing April, I could not let her go when we were having so many days of rain. So, I made arrangements for the vet to come on Sunday afternoon.

This way, April could spend Saturday outside in the sunshine, which was her favorite thing to do. She could spend her last day up on the hill (we have twenty acres), exploring our property like she always did. And of course, she would eat lots of chop meat and cookies.

But I soon knew this could not wait. I would have to call the veterinarian early Friday morning. Sadly, April would miss out on her beautiful day! But God intervened. Instead of rain, on

Friday morning the sun was out. It was beautiful! I knew this was His way of letting me know I had to let her go right away. Acting on that "knowing," I called the vet early Friday morning. To my relief, he agreed to come after office hours in the afternoon.

This way, April received hugs and kisses all day, *sooooooooo* much chop meat and cookies. And she walked out in the back of the house where she loved to walk and sniff. She even got to run a bit and pose for pictures by the short Christmas trees!

After all this, April came in, laid by the front door in the sunshine, and seemed so calm. She knew, I knew, we all knew…God gave us a bright sunny day for her to enjoy with us before she left this world.

To make this passing even more special, I asked Ziggi and Rusty, my friends' doggies to help April as she was passing over. It worked! It meant so much that two brindle greyhounds helped my brindle, April.

 April laid in the sunshine when she got a shot to make her sleepy and relaxed, then she passed calmly.

Her beauty and love were fantastic gifts that will remain with me forever. Her ashes will be put out in back of the house with our other greyhounds—our own little 'pet cemetery'—where she and Poe and Bree are resting.

As much as it hurts to lose our beloved pets, their gift to us far outweighs the pain. Love, devotion, joy, playfulness, adoration, forgiveness. I think that is why 'dog' is 'God' spelled backwards!

Nancy's story is an inspiration to me. As I read it, I remember that we can "know" when our animals are ready to go if we open our hearts. As we tune into our love for them, we can figure out how to make their last day one of misty-eyed, heartfelt memories for ourselves and them.

10

TRANSITION TIME

> Now is never the right time to lose an animal.
>
> — MARIBETH DECKER

ONCE YOU'VE MADE the decision to release them from their body, now's the time to use the Energetic Green Smoothie I wrote about earlier in this book. This way, you can be certain you're connected to your animals. Relax and trust that your information is getting through. Your heart will open wide if you allow it to, and the information will flow to your animal. If you need to, watch my YouTube video and practice a little bit.

When it's time, tell your animal it's time for them to leave their bodies so they don't hurt anymore. They're going to feel so much better once they do. Assure them not to worry. You love them, and you are taking care of them right to the end.

If you can, do something with your animal that they'll absolutely love! Is there anything your animal might like? Treats they can't usually eat? Visits from friends and family? Whatever you can muster up will help you smile when you remember that day.

Also, it's time to get your animal's final wishes. Ask them if they'd like something special when they transition. Who should be there? Where should it be? What *don't* they want? The key is to accept whatever pops in. Go with it if you can. Don't second guess them or yourself. You'll be glad you did! This memory will be one of your favorites when you think of your animal's last day.

Finally, explain to your other animals what's going to happen or has happened. You can assume they already noticed some dramatic, downhill changes for the one who is transitioning. But you can be more explicit and explain that since their buddy isn't having fun anymore, you're going to help them. You'll be sad because they aren't around anymore, but we'll have each other. And be clear that just because one animal isn't around anymore, it doesn't mean you're getting rid of them.

~

Peanut: Taking a Walk

Peanut with Genesis. Photo credit: Patrick Coye.

My son Pat's dog, Peanut the Pit Bull, had finally succumbed to the last stages of her chronic kidney disease. Pat scheduled a date for the veterinarian to come to the house to release Peanut from her body.

Peanut's last day was a dreary, rainy, chilly day. It didn't matter. Pat took Peanut to the Belle View Marina in Alexandria, Virginia, one of her favorite hangouts. He put her in a kid's wagon and wrapped her up to keep her comfy. Pat, Genesis, and daughter Hailee pulled her through the nature trail—Peanut smiled ear to ear, so happy to be there. My husband, our dogs, and I walked with them. Lucky for me, the rain hid my tears. Then we went back to Patrick's house to await the veterinarian.

11

HELPING CHILDREN THROUGH THEIR ANIMAL'S DEATH

“ For most kids, pets are more than just animals their families own—they're members of the family and the best of friends.

— *WHEN A PET DIES*, NEMOURS CHILDREN'S HEALTH

HOW DO we deal with the death of our animals in light of our children's wellbeing? It's important to think of our kids and how to help them process the death of someone they loved.

My children loved our animals and were very sad when they died. I have a memory of my son Pat holding his teddy bear hamster, ChiChi, after he just died. Pat was crying his eyes out.

We always had a funeral for the small animals (birds, hamsters, rats) and buried them on our property. The kids would find a box to put them in and decorate it. We would bury the box and say some good words about how we loved our animal. Sometimes my daughter Andrea would put flowers on the grave.

For the dogs, we always talked to the children about what our dog's physical condition was. We explained why and when we were going to release them from their bodies. We brought home the dogs' ashes afterward.

When my granddaughter Hailee asked what the veterinarian was going to do with Peanut's body, I told the truth but tempered it somewhat. I explained the veterinarian would put Peanut's body in a very hot place so that it would turn to ashes. I then reminded her that Peanut wasn't in the body anymore; she was in Heaven. Her family would get Peanut's ashes back from the veterinarian as another way to remember her.

These simple acts acknowledged and honored our children's grief and love for their animals. It also provided them with an example that adults consider animal lives and deaths seriously. I think it helped my children become compassionate adults towards the people and animals that have come into their lives.

This useful advice, reprinted with permission from the wonderful folks at helpguide.org[55] provides accurate, heartfelt information for parents:

> The loss of an animal may be your child's first experience of death—and your first opportunity to teach them about coping with the grief and pain that inevitably accompanies the joy of loving another living creature. Losing a pet can be a traumatic experience for any child. Many kids love their pets very deeply and some may not even remember a time in their life when the pet wasn't around. A child may feel angry and blame themselves—or you—for the pet's death. A child may feel scared that other people or animals they love may also leave them. How you handle the grieving process can determine whether the experience has a positive or negative effect on your child's personal development.
>
> Some parents feel they should try to shield their children from the sadness of losing a pet by either not talking about the pet's death, or by not being honest about what's happened. Pretending the animal ran away, or "went to sleep," for exam-

ple, can leave a child feeling even more confused, frightened, and betrayed when they finally learn the truth. It's far better to be honest with children and allow them the opportunity to grieve in their own way.

- **Let your child see you express your own grief at the loss of the pet.** If you don't experience the same sense of loss as your child, respect their grief and let them express their feelings openly, without making them feel ashamed or guilty. Children should feel proud that they have so much compassion and care deeply about their animal companions.
- **Reassure your child** that they weren't responsible for the pet's death. The death of a pet can raise a lot of questions and fears in a child. You may need to reassure your child that you, their parents, are not also likely to die. It's important to talk about all their feelings and concerns.
- **Involve your child in the dying process.** If you've chosen euthanasia for your pet, be honest with your child. Explain why the choice is necessary and give the child a chance to spend some special time with the pet and say goodbye in their own way.
- **If possible, give the child an opportunity to create a memento of the pet.** This could be a special photograph, or a plaster cast of the animal's paw print, for example.
- **Allow the child to be involved in any memorial service,** if they desire. Holding a funeral or creating a memorial for the pet can help your child express their feelings openly and help process the loss.
- **Do not rush out to get the child a "replacement pet"** before they've had a chance to grieve the loss they feel. Your child may feel disloyal, or you could send the message that the grief and sadness felt when something dies can simply be overcome by buying a replacement."

12

DURING THE TRANSITION

> Tears shed for another ... are not a sign of weakness.
> They are a sign of a pure heart.
>
> — JOSE N. HARRIS

YOUR ANIMAL'S transition is not a medical procedure. It is a sacred time when a soul passes on. In this chapter, I will share some tips to help you and your animal during the transition.

First and foremost, be with them during the transition. Your presence is comforting. Touch, hold, and talk to them. If you have learned energy healing, use those modalities to help their bodies and souls relax into this new life.

If you can't be with them, don't despair. Be intentional about connecting with them through your heart, maybe using the Energetic Green Smoothie. Send love, talk to them in your mind, and see them relaxing as they realize you're with them in spirit.

Even in unexpected deaths, animals may reach out to you and connect for comfort. Most of us don't realize this. Our souls are always available to those we love. Can you feel the truth of that statement? If they reach out to us, we respond on a level that lets them know we love them even in this terrible moment. Remember that friends, family, and even good spirits will come around to help them through the transition.

Consider bringing the veterinarian to your house. This lessens your animal's anxiety with being at the veterinary office when they pass. If you're lucky, your veterinarian will also treat this as a sacred duty. When my grand-dog Peanut passed, her veterinarian treated each step the same way an ordained person would do during a ritual of their faith. She moved slowly, sat quietly, and even wrapped Peanut's body gently in the blanket to be cremated. Even in death, she treated this body with respect for the life it had held. She was a calming presence in this sacred event.

Invite local family members. Ask neighbors and their animals, especially if they had a relationship, to stop by before the sacred ceremony begins. Even neighborhood kids, who love your animal, and their parents could come by. Tell favorite stories about your wonderful animal. It's like a wake with your animal still around.

Tell your animal it's okay to go and that you'll survive the pain and remember the good times. Assure your animal that you'll be fine. They don't have to stick around so you don't feel the pain of loss. You love them more than that. "I'm doing what's best for you, my cherished animal. Because I love you so much," (in your own words) can be your guiding mantra.

I always do a bit of additional preparation by telling them that *before* their body dies, they should step up and out of it like they would step out of the house, the car, or the barn. I figure, why wait? Skip the last part and move on. I ask them to imagine they are on their way to their next life with ease and grace.

If you're up to it, tune into when they leave their body. When my son's dog Peanut the Pit Bull (I love saying that) had received her first euthanasia shot, I felt a shift in the energy. I asked my son Pat if he felt it, too. He did! We knew Peanut had transitioned even though her body was still shutting down.

One client told me that during the euthanasia process, she was suddenly filled with the most heart-warming joy! She knew her dog had burst through bonds of her physical body and back into the light-ness of her spirit body. Another client stated that one of their dog's soul had left his body a day or two before it finally shut down. Amaz-ing, but I felt the truth of that statement.

Please, if you feel or "know" something just happened, accept the gift of being that connected. It doesn't happen to all of us all the time. But, it's worth being aware of this lovely possibility. It will be another memory that can soothe your grief as you heal.

When people find out I'm retired Navy, they sometimes thank me for my service. This works for your animal's body, too. The body has its own consciousness separate from your animal's soul or spirit. If you doubt this, think about how many systems are working every single second to keep you and your animal alive. We don't have to constantly command our bodies to breathe, blink, swallow, eat, digest, eliminate, move messages back and forth along the nervous system, or activate antibodies. The body does it so we can live our lives.

So specifically thank your animal's body for hanging in there. Tell it how grateful that it held your beloved animal's spirit as long as it could. Doing this assists the body to let go as the soul is letting go. There's something sweet about saying all this to the body. This quote from the Bible, although it wasn't meant for this purpose, still feels like a perfect way to acknowledge the body's work: "Well done, good and faithful servant" from Matthew 25:23. And, continue to say, "Rest. Your job here is finally done. Thank you."

Feel the body relax—maybe imagine a deep sigh of "Oh thank you!" coming from the body. You are releasing it from service to this wonderful soul so it can return to Mother Earth/Gaia.

It is really wonderful to set up a welcoming party from the other side to attend the transition. All you have to do is ask. Invite the family and friends they love who have passed on, both human and animal. And, if there are people or animals they never met, but love you, invite them too!

Visualize a heartfelt reunion. Even though some of them didn't meet your animal in the physical realm, they will still come to welcome your animal. Request they ensure it's a joyous occasion for your animal. Picture an actual party if it makes you smile.

You might also ask whoever is a leader personality to "show them the ropes" of living in the afterlife. It may not be necessary; they were probably already going to be there. But, I guarantee, it will comfort you. Plus, those on the other side love a personal invitation!

If you notice some physical agitation as they transition, create a vibration of love in your whole body and hold them in love. Remind them that it's going to get really fun and light. They're going to feel so much better very soon.

13

AFTER THE TRANSITION

66 Death is only passing through God's other door.

— EDGAR CAYCE

IF YOU CAN, take time off to mourn the loss of your animal. You're probably feeling sick to your soul, so ask for a few days off. Being sick at heart is still being sick, so take sick leave or personal leave it if feels right. This will give you time to center yourself before you have to be a useful, functioning human being again. Don't just push your grief down and ignore it. It could "rear its ugly head" later.

Most animals who pass have an easy transition. They understand their new energy body quickly and get on with enjoying it. The Rainbow Bridge is a lovely way of understanding this. They run free and play full-time without fear.

Some animals find it harder to transition to a light-filled energetic body, though. They take a bit longer to move from their physical bodies to joyful freedom. These animals need time to acclimate to their energy body. I've had a sense that these animals enter a "rehabilitation" phase. I see them tucked in by loving beings who have old-time nurses' uniforms, hats and all. These animals may have had an unexpected transition (like an accident). Or, they may have had so many physical ailments that it takes a while to fully reclaim their energetic body after they pass.

And, there's special healing for aggressive animals (usually dogs in my experience) who were let go from this life because they weren't safe with people or animals. Sacred beings work with them to help them finally become that trusting, loving soul we sensed when they were part of our lives.

CONNECTING WITH THEM AFTER THEY'VE PASSED

Connecting with your deceased animal telepathically uses the same process as with live animals. I'd just be thoughtful and ask if it's a good time to connect. Maybe they've got a full social calendar now!

You'll probably need to allow your grief to dissipate some before you try to connect. That's because strong grief and feelings of remorse, guilt, and anger are like physical barriers to the connection. One way to move beyond those harsh feelings is to send good energy and prayers. If it feels right to you, prayers for a safe passage to their next place are always useful. Or, you could send love while remembering how they enhanced your life. This is good medicine for you and them! It helps them settle in as they realize they don't have a physical body anymore.

MEMORIALS AND SHRINES

If you're grieving for your animal, create a memorial to focus the love you feel into something tangible: A table or shelf with their pictures, ashes, a favorite toy, and maybe their collar. A memorial is "something that keeps remembrance alive." A shrine to remember your animal honors your relationship. Doing something positive gives you an outlet for your grief and love.

My love for my animals runs deep, and the love is mutual. Through their love and support, I remember I'm lovable. That's profound. If that's true for you, then the loss of that being in your life is significant. Creating a memorial helps heal that loss.

Remember, grieving for your animal is not trivial! Memorials and shrines can be excellent ways to honor their importance in your life.

~

Nibbles: One family honored their guinea pig's transition

Nibbles. Photo credit: Regina D.

Nibbles, a friendly guinea pig, lived with his human family, rabbits Bobby and Munch, and chickens Belle, Sally, and Ella. While Nibbles belonged to Matthew, he was also really loved by the whole family. Nibbles enjoyed hanging out in the kitchen where the family gathered and walked up to family members before sitting on their feet.

Nibbles started getting weaker for no reason, so I had a lovely remote session with Nibbles and Regina. Nibbles explained why eating and drinking were difficult, and guinea pig and human shared their love for each other.

Regina had an intuitive hit early Sunday morning that Nibbles had passed. I got a sense of it as well that Sunday morning because I had done late-night healing for him. Bobby the Bunny, who lived right next to Nibbles, was with him when he passed. Before passing, Nibbles laid on a rug a lot. Now Bobby visits the rug often. Munch, the second bunny, went into Nibbles' cage to say his good-byes.

Since Nibbles roamed freely in the house, he would greet family as they entered the home and room. The family missed the joy his greeting gave them. After Nibbles' transitioned, it felt weird for the family to cook without him or feel him under their feet; his shenanigans became a treasured memory.

The family had a funeral for Nibbles. Each family member wrote a letter to Nibbles, telling him how much they loved him. Before the funeral started, Regina photocopied the letters and put them in a folder they called "Nibble Notes." At the funeral, they buried Nibbles in his bed and put the letters on top of his body like a blanket. Even the chickens can visit Nibbles back there!

Nibbles' grave. Photo credit: Regina D.

The Friday before Nibbles passed, Matthew drew a picture of Nibbles. After Nibbles passed, Regina framed the drawing and put it on a table where Nibbles' cage had been along with flowers and rocks.

Nibbles' shrine. Photo credit: Regina D.

~

HOLD A REMEMBRANCE CELEBRATION

We all have different ways of coping with loss. A wonderful idea is to invite family and friends to remember and celebrate your animal's life. Here's how Liz and her husband celebrated their dog Gustav after he died:

When we lost our almost eight-and-half-year-old dog Gustav

just six days after being diagnosed with B-cell lymphoma, my husband and I were in shock as well as in deep grief. Gustav had been a cherished member of our family for six-and-a-half-years.

Because Gustav's death was so sudden, my husband and I figured everyone who knew him would be shocked and saddened too. So, we decided to throw a party at our home to celebrate his life on what would have been his eight-and-half-year-old birthday, which was a month after his passing. I put together a collage of pictures of Gustav's adventures from both coasts that served as the invitation.

We invited friends, neighbors, his vets, his dog walker, his "Houndhosters" family, who took him into their home when-ever we traveled, and the sales associates from all the stores he regularly frequented. And, of course, we had several of his dog friends too.

Both of his vets came, and I shared your (Maribeth's) message from him that he hid his illnesses as long as he could. They appreciated hearing that and agreed he did a masterful job.

For my husband and me, it was a wonderful event because we felt the joy Gustav had brought to others, as well as to us. And it was so comforting to be around people from all walks of life who knew and loved him.

Because I frequently wrote about or referenced Gustav in my work blogs, I also devoted one of my blog posts and a newsletter to some of the many life lessons I learned from Gustav. Writing it helped me clarify how important he had been to me professionally as well as a member of our family.

My writing touched a nerve with many others too. I was so touched by all the comments people made, saying how much they enjoyed reading about his adventures and reflecting on his wisdom. Others shared memories of dogs and cats who had been important in their lives, which also helped me deal with my grief.

Just the other day my husband and I acknowledged what would have been Gustav's ninth birthday. We still miss him so, yet we are so thankful for all we did together in his short life with us.

Whatever you do, do it thoughtfully and with love. It will help you find peace when you're grieving for your animal. They appreciate being remembered with love.

14

VISITS AFTER DEATH

66 The after-death physical manifestations of dogs and cats to their human companions point to other realities beyond this mortal plane.

— DR. MICHAEL W. FOX

WE KNOW love between souls does not die when bodies die. Many of us have heard stories about human family members coming back to let their family know they are okay. So, what about animals?

I am now sure animals visit us as well. Animal visits after death are not uncommon. That's because I've heard so many stories! Don't expect them to be by your side every waking moment after they pass. They might do that for you, but it keeps them from fully moving on to their next phase of life. It keeps you stuck, too. It's like a parent who holds on too tightly to their adult child.

This is a new chapter in your life and theirs. Turn the page to this new chapter and see what will unfold for both of you. Remember, they're part of your soul family. You will never lose them.

Ask them to come and go as they please. Then they're doing it out of pure love rather than obligation. If you need them for support through a tough time, definitely ask them. I know they'll be there.

Be alert to their presence! Here are some examples, which were related to me by sane, intelligent human beings:

- The cat jumped on the bed and snuggled next to her person as she was sleeping.
- Their animal came into a dream and were very present. They weren't just a dream character.
- The person felt their dog sit on their feet like they used to when he was on the planet.
- Humans often report hearing barks or meows.
- Other humans hear nails on the floor as if their animal was walking across the room.
- Someone felt like an animal was licking their face—but their face wasn't wet.
- The person just knew/felt their animal was with them.

WONDERFUL, TRUE STORIES

Here are some personal stories from my family and clients to get you in the groove so you notice when your animal visits you after they pass.

Timmie: Comes to Visit

I was in the Navy and stationed in Pearl Harbor when we found Timmie at a Saint Timothy Church potluck in Aiea, Hawaii. It was clear he was a street puppy, so we took him home. His full name was Saint Timothy of Aiea. Timmie was a true Navy family member, moving with us from Honolulu to Albany, New York, then San Francisco, California, and finally, Washington, DC.

Timmie passed on after we moved to the Washington, DC, area, and I mourned him deeply. Sometime in 2007, after I became a Reiki

Master and a Quantum Touch® practitioner, I was in the kitchen at the stove.

Out of the corner of my eye, I saw Timmie, grinning, with his usual one ear up, one ear down. It was as if he was sitting there looking at me, same as in this picture! I whipped my head to the dining room and yell excitedly, "Timmie!" But, he was gone from view.

I now knew animals survive death. They love us enough to come back and let us know they're doing well.

∽

Eddy: Travels with Me on the Plane

Eddy. Photo credit: Maribeth Decker.

Eddy was a loving girl (named by the kids), a stray for whom we could not find the guardian. So, we kept her.

We had to finally let her go in 2008. The timing was terrible as it was a couple of days before an out-of-town business meeting I was scheduled to staff. I was devastated. I wasn't sure how I was going to be able to staff the meeting with such a heavy heart.

As the plane took off, I felt Eddy's presence in the aisle next to me. People must have thought I was nuts because I was petting her as she sat by my side in the aisle. And, she visited me in my hotel room that night. She had died, but made her presence known to comfort me. Because of her thoughtful, comforting presence, I made it through the meeting.

∽

Ashley: Sunspots in Gail's Office

Ashley, a beautiful Australian Shepherd, was Gail's constant companion. You know the type. Where's Ashley? Find Gail and you've got your answer!

As you may recall from earlier in the book, Ashley was clearly failing when Gail was on a business trip. Gail asked me to connect to Ashley and ask her to hold on until Gail returned home. (This is always an *ask*, not a *demand*. Sometimes their bodies or souls just can't continue.)

In this case, Ashley was able to grant Gail's request. Happily, Gail made it home in time to be with Ashley when she passed. They spent three weeks of quality time together, while Gail readied herself for Ashley's loss. What a gift!

Still, Gail's sorrow was deep and unyielding. Imagine Gail's delight one day when she got a quick glance of Ashley's rear end going into another room! After that, Gail started feeling Ashley's presence in her office. She sometimes hears Ashley while she's working in her office or sitting in the sun. Sitting in the sun was one of Ashley's favorite things to do.

Gail felt so comforted by being able to discern how Ashley makes her presence known.

Callie: Lets Izzy Know

Mary reports that Callie also made her presence known through her horse friend, Izzy. Sometimes when Mary and Izzy were together, Izzy would make a laughing sound that only Callie made. Izzy never made it. We believe that was Callie's way of telling Mary she is visiting.

Izzy recently passed and I anticipate that Mary will have new stories about how both Izzy and Callie contact her!

Harry: Messy Visits

I recently checked in with Harry, a lovely corgi, because his family wanted to see how he was doing after his transition. When I asked

him how he would let his people know he was visiting, he said he had been hanging around the water bowl.

"Seriously?" I thought. "Wouldn't you rather hang out by the food bowl?"

"Nope, the water bowl," Harry confirmed.

Harry aka Harrison Llewellyn. Photo credit: Lillis Werder.

I shared this insight with his people, expecting a "Huh?" But they said that made so much sense. Harry *loved* his water bowl. He loved playing in it as well as kiddie pools. Later that day, I received this email from Lillis, Harry's mom:

I feel good closure now knowing Harry is happy and that he felt so loved. We have been alerted to the water bowl. Today, [my son] Sam and I went to Costco and when we came home, we found two places with water. One was in Sam's room. We were replacing a throw rug earlier today in his room and his hardwood floor had been perfectly dry. When we came home, he found a small puddle of water near the rug. Several inches long.

We also found a long stream of water near the big water bowl in the laundry room. Our dog Sophie had been in her crate, so it was not her doing. And our other dog, Gracie is a neat drinker. We suspect the water was from Harry. We hope it was. I want him to visit us wherever he wants.

~

Cynder: Naughty Behavior

I worked with Renee's dog, Cynder, off and on throughout her life. Cynder was a mischievous dog, sometimes barking through the fence just to see if she could get a rise out of the people or dogs who passed by.

When I chided her for upsetting people and dogs, she told me she was having fun and didn't want to stop. She found their reactions amusing. Yup, that was Cynder. Stirring up a little trouble when she could!

After Cynder passed, Renee called me with another funny story about Cynder. Turns out Cynder visited with her foster mom, Shana, the exact time she was transitioning.

Cynder. Photo credit: Renee Greenwell.

Shana had fostered Cynder for a year before Renee and her husband Richard adopted her. Cynder wanted to make sure Shana knew she was around by nipping Shana's dog Alice on the butt. That was so in line with Cynder's personality!

∾

Yogi Bear: Help Needed

Natalie came to me to help her young dog, Spudsky. We veered off course when I asked her about her recently deceased dog, Yogi Bear. Spudsky was okay with this because he knew Natalie was having a hard time releasing her grief.

Yogi Bear. Photo credit: Natalie T.

Natalie shared a painful dream she had about Yogi after he died. Yogi seemed very anxious in her dream, something she hadn't expected. I was also surprised. She was so worried about him. When we checked with Yogi, it turned out that his transition had been a difficult one. He sought Natalie because he completely trusted her. Turns out, this was not just a dream. It really was Yogi, and he was really having a tough time when he reached out to Natalie.

The good news was Natalie, through her love, helped Yogi easily complete his transition. The last time I checked in with him, he was okay and was being looked after by some blessed ethereal beings.

Through her love, Natalie was an energy healer for Yogi!

∾

It's Your Turn

Before reading this book, maybe you weren't attuned to animals visiting us after death, even if you've heard about people's spirits visiting members of your family (or if you've experienced it yourself). Maybe you didn't even realize animal visits after death were a possibility. Now you know.

Liberate yourself! Ask your animals to contact you with a vibration full of love. You can do that by thinking of a memory that warms your heart! If you see or hear them, don't chalk it up to imagination.

When your cat, who has no physical body anymore, jumps on the bed to sleep with you, trust that he did. If you dreamed your dog visited with you after she died, assume you actually spent time with her. How lucky to enjoy each other's company! Treasure the experience. Don't explain it away with the excuse that you were just missing them. If your beloved animal goes to the trouble of making their presence known by visiting you, honor that expression of love.

Because once you allow that gift to sink into your heart, something changes within you.

Life becomes softer and sweeter, and this experience takes away some of the sting of death. It gives a delicious memory, which is a balm for our beat-up hearts. We don't stop missing them, but the grief starts to lessen. We know they love us even after their passing.

15

LINGERING QUESTIONS

> Individuals do not meet by chance. They are necessary
> in the experiences of others, though they may not
> always use their opportunities in a spiritual way or
> manner.

— EDGAR CAYCE

AS AN ANIMAL COMMUNICATOR who has helped countless animals' transition and supported their families through the process, people have asked their animals some tough questions. Maybe some of these will help you find greater peace over the loss of your animal. As you read these questions, notice if you're getting any "Ahas"! Don't discount the first thought or feeling that comes to you—that could be the straight-up intuitive gift from your animal, especially if it resonates with you.

WHY DID THEY LEAVE?

We should consider this question from two viewpoints: What our *animal's* spiritual needs were and what *our* spiritual needs were during our time together.

I see both sides because animals have their own purpose in life, and it's not simply to help us out. On a soul level, they choose a life that would help them become closer to the lovely being Creator knows them to be. So, what did they come here to learn? What was their goal in this life? As sentient beings with the potential for enlightenment, did they desire to learn a specific lesson? To complete something left undone? To grow in a specific area? This is hard for us to grasp. Most of us aren't brought up to think that animals might desire spiritual growth or enlightenment.

Then we can ask, what were we to learn from living with them? What gift did they bring us? To teach patience? To fill a certain need only they could fill because of who they were? To show us how to love and care for someone depending on us?

If you believe our lives are purposeful, and we're here to learn and grow into better human beings, then think of our animal companions as an integral part of our spiritual journey. Their lives are like chapters in our Book of Life, and our lives are chapters in their Books of Life. They chose us and we chose them. Their personalities, challenges, and love contribute to helping us move forward spiritually if we choose.

This has been an incredibly hard question for me to answer in my own life. Nine years after he passed, my dog Mitsubishi explained more clearly what his purpose was in my life, and why he left when he did.

The best I can understand as I write this book is that we play both the student and the teacher for each other. Given that analogy, the tough animal challenges in our lives might be the equivalent of signing up for graduate courses. Alternately, it could be remedial education for those of us who aren't getting the message about something we need to improve. They say when the Creator wants you to know something, the message starts as a tap on the shoulder, then a whisper, and maybe becomes a shout. If you're incredibly deaf to the communication, life delivers the equivalent of a two-by-four—something you can't ignore. Maybe the tough animal challenges are our wake-up calls.

When animals have accidents or other circumstances that led to sudden death, or they have sicknesses or chronic issues that led to an earlier-than-expected death, I believe this is when we are the gift to our animals.

I believe abrupt endings are decisions of their Higher Self saying, "I received so much love, it was just what I needed to heal, thank you, I love you so much." These endings are not meant to bring guilt over what we've done or haven't done.

Instead, your animals received care and love that was instrumental in healing a psychic or spiritual wound of the past. It might have been in the life you shared with them or a prior lifetime. You demonstrated through your heartfelt love and actions that they were lovable and worth the effort. In fact, they were worth going above and beyond. You affirmed the value of their soul in this incarnation.

TIMING

I choose to believe the animal's Higher Self decides when's the right time to go—even when they die unexpectedly. The Higher Self is more than the animal we interact with daily. The individual we interact with daily is what I call their personality—the one who expresses their "dog-ness" or "cat-ness" or "hamster-ness" through their peculiarities and preferences. It's how they see the world and how they respond to daily life.

Their Higher Self is that being we sometimes experience behind their loving eyes. The expanded consciousness that knows they chose us as much as we chose them. The self who knows us on a deeper, more spiritual level. The self that is part of our Soul Family throughout eternity.

REAL LIFE STORIES ABOUT TIMING

Below are stories of what I gleaned about why animals left when they did. Maybe you will resonate with one of these and notice that it might be true for you and your animal.

Looking Ahead and Saying No

In some cases when our animals die unexpectedly, they had taken a peek at their future path and said, "Nope. Not going there." They decided it's time to move on.

Sometimes animals have a sense that a budding physical diagnosis is going to get much worse in the near future. Their people may have learned about the diagnosis, too—but not always. Their animal makes a unilateral decision to skip that "downward spiral/tons of medical interventions" phase altogether and find a quick death.

Another Way of Saying No: Hiding Their Diagnosis

I've met animals who seemed to hide their diagnosis until it was too late for meaningful medical interventions. Their people took them to numerous veterinarians, who couldn't figure out what was wrong. So, their death wasn't a result of their human's neglectful actions. To the contrary, their people were diligent in seeking out medical assistance for their beloved animal. Once the animals got a correct diagnosis, they did not stay in their bodies for very long. They just didn't want to put themselves or their people through any more suffering.

∽

James: I Got What I Needed

In one case, a relatively young dog James passed from a disease. He wanted the chance to be fully loved and cared for by a human being, even though the pup could be considered "good for nothing" in the utilitarian human sense. My sense was that in a past life, he wasn't valued when he stopped being able to help hunt for food or perform a certain chore. In that life, there was no mourning his ending; he was just a tool that stopped being useful. He was discarded.

In this lifetime, his illness required an ongoing expenditure of time and money. Thankfully, his family loved James for who he was during his short life. This loving connection was an extraordinary healing gift from his human, Emily. James' life was short but filled with love. Emily loved James for who he was, not for what he could do for her and her family.

James got what he needed and moved on. He graduated from this particular curriculum of life.

~

Rhyuu: I Want to be with You When I Pass

My sister-in-law Barbie found Rhyuu (pronounced Roo) on Craig's List. She was six weeks old. Barbie drove an hour each way to bring Rhyuu home. Barbie soon discovered that Rhyuu's esophagus had been crushed when a child choked her.

Barbie and her vet gave Rhyuu the best care possible, but she was unable

Rhyuu. Photo credit: Barbie Sturgis.

to keep food down and the esophagus was not healing. As Rhyuu continued to worsen, Barbie made the tough decision to put Rhyuu down six weeks later.

I was kept updated on Rhyuu and sent loving energy, but my intuition said she was not going to make it. I believe Rhyuu called out to Barbie and her family for love, and Barbie responded. They were the right souls to help her pass feeling loved and treasured.

Barbie tells me Rhyuu taught her patience. Barbie said, "It would have been very easy to get angry and yell at her for the constant mess and three-or-four-times-a-day bath we had to give her. She couldn't help it, so I learned a whole lot of patience. Many times, I wanted to just give up and pass her on to Lee or the kids, but I stuck by her side. The last day of her life, Rhyuu just wanted to sleep. Every now and then, she'd look at me and I knew it was time to let go. I called Lee and we took her to the vet. She is buried in a special flower garden with her bed and her toys, leash, and halter. It is called Rhyuu's Bed."

Barbie passed too early, too. I am sure an "all grown up" Rhyuu was there to greet her and help her find her way in the next world.

Every person who takes in an ailing animal and cares for it, allowing it to know your love and patience, is doing (dare I say it?) Creator/Spirit's work. And, what goes around comes around. Thank you.

~

Mitsubishi: Earth Angel

Mitsubishi came into my family's life shortly after my first husband Winston died, so you can imagine how special Mitsubishi was to me. The kids helped me pick him out. A Siberian Husky, he was six months old when we got him. I told myself he was passed over for so long because he didn't have blue eyes. Instead, I now think he was doing whatever it took to stick around until I showed up.

Mitsubishi. Photo credit: Maribeth Decker.

Mitsu (also known as "Bishi Boy") was a handful. He loved to run. He was always getting away from us so he could run. (Yes, I had taken him to a dog trainer, in case you're wondering!) He was single-minded. When I was walking in the neighborhood after I had recently convinced Mitsu to come home with me, a young girl told me she saw a "wolf" running in the woods behind her house! I had to laugh and say, "No, that was my Bishi Boy being naughty again."

Mitsu was a wonderful companion and my emotional support dog. Even after I remarried, he and I had a special relationship, which included running together through lots of different neighborhoods.

Mitsubishi had a couple of health scares when he was about eleven, but he came back from them with flying colors. I was so glad because he got to enjoy the DC area's "Snowmaggedon" in 2010. By 2012, he was unable to walk after some very bad seizures, so we brought him home to die. We had a vet come out after a wonderful day of saying goodbye.

When I became more proficient at communicating with animals, I asked him why he had to leave. He was very stern and said, "You had me long enough. Somebody else needed you."

And, in fact, someone else did need me. We had adopted Tibor, a rescue dog, a couple of months after Mitsu died. Tibor had major fear and aggression issues, although you wouldn't know it now. My family was able to love him back to his sweet, companionable self. The real Tibor.

What did Tibor do for me? Tibor pushed me into developing my animal communication skills. My other animals had connected with me, but I was not paying attention. When I started seeing a vision of a dog biting a man's arm every time I sat down next to Tibor, I knew I had to get animal communication training!

We've come to believe that Tibor was a bait dog for fighting and was being taught how to be a guard dog. Problem is, that's not him. He's a kind soul. So, in addition to needing to help another dog find his best self, it was also time for me to have a new teacher, Tibor, to move me forward on my journey as an animal communicator.

∼

AFTER NOTE: As I taught my UConnect Animal Communication class in 2021, we delved into connecting with animals who had passed on. I heard a further message from Mitsubishi that astounded me. He said that he probably wasn't going to return (reincarnate) again to the Earth. He wasn't a soul who normally incarnated, but he wanted to assist me through the death of my husband, Winston. Mitsu had no plans to return to earth like other animals in my life. He is more comfortable with his ethereal presence. I was blessed to have him. My sense is that he was a light being, maybe an angel, who took on this particular mission. Thanks, Mitsubishi!

∼

Molasses: I Meant to Do That

Susan had a session with me to find peace about how her dog, Molasses, had died. It had been nine months since she had put Molasses down after a serious fall and she still experienced strong grief and guilt.

Molasses had been a great support for Susan after her husband died. But, Molasses understood Susan no longer needed her for that reason and was ready to move on. Both the human and the animal felt constrained by the relationship. It had run its course. Molasses let me see her fall down the stairs indicated her readiness to move on. It was a way to transition that was cleaner than a lingering illness. Susan felt relief with the news and was able to let go of the guilt and much of her grief.

~

Sophie: It's Time for You to Fly

Deb was still distraught about losing her dog Sophie, who had been an excellent companion. Our session started a bit late. Funny enough, the first thing I saw was a cartoon dog with the oversized watch pacing back and forth pointing to her watch. Deb laughed and confirmed Sophie expected punctuality in her schedule.

Sophie. Photo credit: Deb.

Sophie showed me a mother bird pushing the baby bird out of the nest so it could learn to fly. Sophie said it was time for Deb to rely less on Sophie so she could "spread her wings" and fly.

Sophie's companionship had provided Deb with an environment that felt safe. But, in my understanding, it was the equivalent of living with your mom when it was time to be out on your own. Losing Sophie was meant to be a catalyst for Deb to evaluate where she was headed. In Sophie's estimation, Deb should expand into new areas of her life, which turned out to be exploring new areas of work.

Deb got it: She knew exactly what Sophie was saying. She told Sophie she would definitely follow her advice. Deb is currently pursuing a new career that has her very excited!

~

WHAT IF THEY PASSED WHEN WE WEREN'T WITH THEM?

It's so difficult when animals pass when we're not with them. Did we do something wrong? Is it our fault that they chose not to go when we were present?

To find peace, remember their love for us. That didn't change. Instead, the timing is most likely about *their* spiritual growth. Despite their love for us, it may have been easiest for them to leave while we're not present. Maybe they decided to spare us this last difficult decision. They took that decision off our shoulders.

In one case, a client had to take her husband to the emergency room for heart attack symptoms. When they returned home, their dog had passed away. They were heartbroken! When I checked in with their dog, I made a wonderful discovery. Although this woman was not consciously aware of it, her dog felt her presence. Some part of her was with him as he passed on. He felt loved. Her Higher Self was connected to his Higher Self.

In all circumstances, family members and friends (people and animals) who passed are there for our animals. Picture them saying, "Hey, come on, let us show you around your new existence."

HOW DO I MOVE FORWARD?

If you find you're not healing from the loss, seek outside help. Not just for your own wellbeing, but for your animal spirit's wellbeing. Sadly, your unending grief can literally hold your animal back from fully releasing themselves from the physical world and enjoying their next life.

I once tried to help a man who had lost his dog. As he shared his grief, he broke down with huge sobs of pain and loss, recalling his loss. I was astounded when I asked him when his beloved dog had passed. From the amount of grief he exhibited, I was sure his dog had passed less than six months before. Turns out, it was ten years earlier. That's not healthy for him or his dog.

Many shelters have groups for people who are grieving the loss of their animals. These are conducted by people with training in grief counseling. They provide solace in a group setting, which can be healing in and of itself. Your veterinarian may also know some resources you can tap into.

Since this book is written from my own experience in helping animals and people through their transitions, consider working with an animal communicator. There are many good animal communicators, and many, like me, work remotely. So, distance is not an issue.

~

Britney: Inconsolable Grief

Nancy W., from North Carolina, shared the following experience with her own overwhelming grief:

> A dear friend referred me to Maribeth after the passing of my beloved cat, Britney. I had felt an inconsolable grief and a steady stream of tears over those next couple of weeks. It was a grief unlike any I have ever known.
>
> I gained such deep insights as I reconnected with Britney

during my phone call with Maribeth. The session was tremendously healing and comforting. Since our call, a smile comes across my face every time I think of Britney. I feel such peace, joy, and gratitude, instead of deep sorrow and loss.

I'm truly grateful for the special work that comes through Maribeth. What a blessing to have been referred to her by my dear friend.

~

Have the courage and love for you and your animal to seek help. Being able to think of your animal fondly and smile when you remember them is so worth it!

WHAT IF I CAN'T TAKE CARE OF MY ANIMAL ANYMORE?

Sometimes people are the first to transition, or are going into their final stage of life, and are no longer able to take care of their animals. I think about this more as I grow older. Making a plan will bring you comfort that you did right by your animals; it's better than hoping for the best or assuming your family will take care of your animals. The article, *What To Do When You Can't Take Care of Your Pet Anymore*, gives some good advice for when seniors might want to get assistance for caring for their animals.[56]

~

Archie: Brenda's Taking Care of You Now

A woman whose house my friend Brenda cleaned made an agreement with Brenda about the woman's little dog, Archie. Brenda agreed to take in Archie when the woman went into a nursing home. This agreement included a small stipend to cover Archie's expenses. This way, the woman could rest easy because Archie had a home with Brenda, whom he already knew, until he passed away. (*Names changed.*)

~

Robert: You Get to Stay with Family

Janice asked me to communicate with her mother's dog, Robert, as her mother had moved into a hospice setting. Robert had been living with Janice's sister's family, but her mother had made arrangements for Robert to go to another place when she moved to hospice.

When I connected with Robert, I realized immediately that Robert not only understood some of what was happening, but he had real love for his mom. He wanted to know if Mom was in pain because he knew she was sick. I was astounded that Robert was concerned about his mom's pain. He showed a genuine and deep compassion for her. While I had not anticipated that reaction, I should have. Also, Robert was concerned about what was going to happen to him, but that only came out after he found out Mom was okay, even though she wasn't coming home.

Although Mom was alive but not physically with Janice during our session, I felt Mom's presence come through. I would say that it was her Higher Self or her energy connecting with us. I was able to facilitate a three-way discussion between Mom, Robert, and Janice.

Here's what Janice wrote:

Regarding Mom's pain, I shared with the dog what Mom told me: she was a bit uncomfortable physically but was handling it okay. That was a relief to her family. And the discussion about what was going to happen to Robert was heartwarming. Mom did not want to burden her daughters with taking care of Robert now that she couldn't do it.

But, it turns out both the dog and the other daughter found great comfort in each other's presence. He was with Mom's family and she had Mom's dog. A win–win. She affirmed that Robert seemed to fit right in.

During our session, Mom, Janice, and Robert said their goodbyes and shared their love for each other. Mom lived for a good while before she passed, and through this time, she knew that Robert and her daughter were gifts to each other. A way to celebrate Mom's life! (*Names changed.*)

I THINK MY ADOPTED ANIMAL ENDED UP IN THE SHELTER AFTER THEIR PERSON DIED

Maybe you think your adopted animal came from someone who died. Sadly, I've met several (mostly) dogs adopted from shelters who weren't taken in by their human's family after their human died. I received this information when their people asked how they ended up in the shelter.

If you have the sense that your adopted animal came to you because their person died, use the animal communication suggestions I shared earlier in the book. Tell them their person loved them but couldn't take care of them anymore. Assure them you are going to take over to give them the best life ever.

If you're up to it, ask their previous guardian to connect with their animal and tell them the same thing. It might feel like you're making it up, but they're going to be so relieved that you're doing what you can for their beloved animal. I bet they'll do their darnedest to ask their animal to trust you and enjoy their life with you.

16

DOING GOOD WORK
AFTER DEATH

66 There is so much more to learn—what kind of jobs do
our animals have in the afterlife? What does it look like
for them?

— TRISHA MCCAGH, *ANIMAL TALK*

WHEN I FIRST ENCOUNTERED AN ANIMAL HELPING FROM the
other side, I was surprised, though I shouldn't have been. I saw how
Sacred Divine beings helped me assist deceased individuals who were
"stuck" on the earth move on to the light. And, many of us are
comfortable with asking for help from our Creator as well as blessed
beings. So maybe Creator gives animals the ability to assist those who
need it, whether in spirit or still in their physical form.

Make no mistake, though. These are strictly voluntary undertak-
ings by your animals. No animal is forced to do this. No J.O.B.s if they
don't want them. They can enjoy their version of the Rainbow Bridge
as long as they want! The Rainbow Bridge, to me, is where animals
cavort and play like in a Disney movie without any bad stuff happening. So many animals love that. Running, jumping, playing, and

reuniting with the people and animals they love who passed. Yes, it's good.

To embrace this idea, you must get over the beliefs that animals only love us because we feed them and that their highest thinking ability is the equivalent of, "There's a squirrel; it's time to bark!" When you expand your beliefs beyond what most of us have heard growing up, you can begin to see your animal's depth and how they can become a potential source of assistance.

I sense that animals are evolving, participating more consciously in the story of the planet. Or, maybe they were always participating in the story of the planet and we're finally evolved enough to notice. I wonder if someday the lion and the lamb really will lie down together. I would be delighted if the paradigm of predator/prey was finally somehow, past its prime.

I have witnessed a more expanded, visionary personality emerge after an animal dies. My training teaches me that humans have a higher self in addition to our personality and ego; I believe animals also have a higher self, which emerges more fully after death.

You can always ask your animals what they're doing in the afterlife. Many are doing just what you think they'd be up to—running, chasing, snoozing, catching up with old friends, human and animal.

But, there are other possibilities for our animals. For instance, they might take on guardian/protector duties for us after they pass. They could become a spiritual guide, providing insightful information. Or, they show up to comfort us when we're emotionally distraught. People have even reported that one of their animals who passed was helping the newest family member learn the ins and outs of being a good family member: how to act, how not to act, and what brings their people joy. Some animals have been delighted to help their human find the next animal companion for the family; people have reported feeling guided by their animal in spirit to their next companion. Some animals will return to help another animal transition.

STORIES OF ANIMALS HELPING AFTER THEY PASSED

I shared with one husband and wife that their recently passed female dog was nursing puppies who had died young. Interestingly, they told me her background story included giving birth to puppies who were taken from her too soon!

Another dog in spirit was helping people here on earth whose job it is to help find and free people involuntary caught up in sex trafficking.

I told another woman that her dog was doing something similar— finding lost people. She became extremely excited because as a psychic, she helps authorities find lost people. Now she has her dog helping from the other side! Before you get all skeptical on me, understand that I hadn't known that she did this kind of work before our session.

Some of the animals I have known in life have also assisted me in various ways that, before I started down this path, I would not have imagined was possible. For instance, I have sometimes run into a human in spirit who is stuck and is reluctant to move on. I will ask them if they like dogs. If I get a yes, I ask my dogs in spirit to come and help them move forward into the light. This has worked. My guess is they think, "If the dogs are happy to go to the spiritual realm, it's probably a safe place!" And I have asked my animals and other animals I worked with who've passed to come and greet an animal who's ready to transition.

～

Hiccup: Callie Helps

I have found animals who have been abused/neglected by people tend to lump us into one category: a species not to be trusted.

Callie the horse, having been abused and neglected, has helped me with a rescue miniature mule named Hiccup, who lives at a miniature donkey rescue facility in Pennsylvania. When she was alive, and through her time with Mary, Callie was able to discern there are good humans in addition to mean humans.

I started working remotely with Hiccup. He had been a tough case. For about five months, he absolutely refused to accept medical help for a lung infection—all because of his fear of humans.

What's so lovely about this rescue organization is that they were unwilling to force treatment on him. They believed trust does not come through forced interactions.

After I started working remotely with Hiccup, he allowed the humans who worked at the rescue to give him the antibiotics to clear his lung infection. Still, Hiccup felt skittish around humans.

Callie helped Hiccup learn there are good humans on this planet he can trust. Hiccup is getting friendlier with the people at the facility and finding life enjoyable. Finally!

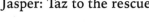

Jasper: Taz to the rescue

Jasper. Photo credit: Tammy Comstock.

Jasper was a tenacious cat. He had been diagnosed with hyperthyroidism but was adamant that he would not be given his meds. His early life as a feral cat made it difficult to submit to human interactions like this. I remotely provided Jasper with an infusion of energy on a weekly basis for over a year, but there came a time when his body had run out of gas. Tammy found him lying very still and obviously close to death. She called me to see if he was ready. I checked in and he was. Even more so, his body was ready.

Tammy asked me to help Jasper transition from his body. As I checked in, he was having second thoughts. I heard him say, "No! No!

No!" At the same time, Tammy reported to me that he was shaking his head even after a second sedative was given to him by his very kind veterinarian.

I reminded Jasper that his body could no longer hold him. I told Jasper that his body was done-done-done. At that point, his best buddy, Taz (who had already passed), stepped up to help. I saw Taz nuzzle and lick Jasper as he told Jasper he was going to love this new life. Jasper finally let go.

I was so surprised when Jasper turned into a small kitten and one of the light beings with us shifted into a mommy kitty to nurse Jasper through his recovery. You see, Jasper's physical decline had also taken a toll on his energy body. Letting him become a kitten for a time, instead of the big, fierce orange cat, allowed him to relax and be nurtured. (P.S. When we checked on Jasper a bit of time after he passed, he was back to being his big orange self.)

~

If you like the idea of your animals in spirit helping you and others in tough times, here are a few ideas to connect more often:

- Ask your animals who've passed to come to you in a time of need. Connect and thank them again. Assure them you'd like their assistance whenever they think they could help.
- Sit quietly and ask if any of your animals are assisting you right now. Ask who it is and what they're doing.
- Ask if any of your animals are doing a job that is beyond you personally. Are they assisting someone or something in the world today? Are they assisting other souls who have passed? Be open, don't evaluate. Enjoy what you get.

17

REINCARNATION

" Souls from the same soul family reunite in the physical realm because they share the same divine purpose. They help each other to complete their spiritual mission.

— WALTER JONES, PSYCHICBLAZE.COM

MOST OF US have heard about reincarnation of humans, but usually not animals. Belief in reincarnation isn't a requirement for connecting to your animals, but it's an interesting belief that can be comforting. [Note: If this doesn't work for you, please skip this section and move on. Don't miss the comforting information for you throughout this book. You deserve to find peace over the loss of your animal.]

I had a profound spiritual experience when I was about twelve years old that created a foundation of belief within me about God or Creator. I asked God if God truly existed and got a personal answer. Astounding! From that time on, I knew that Creator is a loving, caring, and intelligent being. Creator cares for us personally.

So, it never made much sense to me that a loving God gave us one life to figure out how to be good. I mean, God knows humans pretty well. We tend to get off course in being the best people we can be. This happens a lot.

Then, based on our performance, we get sent to The Good Place (or not) forever.

The Creator who came to me loves their Creation. Creator wants to see humans become the enlightened souls we were meant to be. If it takes a while, a *loooong* while, it's okay. Creator is extremely patient. Thank God! So, reincarnation resonated with my personal experience of God.

SOUL FAMILIES

Reincarnation includes a belief that a soul exists before they are born and survives death. Soul families are a tribe of souls who come back to earth together to work on issues from past lives.

I hadn't really thought about animals reincarnating and being a part of our soul families—until a couple of animals in my family reminded me of family animals I knew in the past. Plus, I have had sessions with animals who showed me past lives. Other people I have met have remembered a past life with their animals when they did a past life regression.

One question I hear is, "Can people become animals and vice versa?" Some people adamantly oppose this idea. Religions that believe in reincarnation generally believe this is possible. I found a fascinating story about a cobra that reincarnated as a boy named Dala-wong in the village that was close to where it lived.[57]

HOW SOON DO THEY RETURN?

- Beliefs vary from instantaneous to 1,500 years for people. I didn't find much information on animals. But, a student reported that a family member's animal reincarnated and returned almost immediately to the family. My family animals, as far as I can tell, wait years.

- Don't wish for instantaneous returns. They might need or want some down time. It's also a time for you to process your grief.

HOW DO WE KNOW IF THEY'VE RETURNED?

- You want to call them by a previous animal's name.
- Their current name is similar to a previous animal's name.
- You found them the same way as you did your previous animal.
- They look similar.
- They have similar habits.

Don't expect a clone of your animal's previous personality. Let them be who they are in this lifetime. They have a different reason for being here this time around. Also, it's fun to see how they're different and how some of their traits have continued into this life.

If it's possible for you to believe in reincarnation, there are some comforting benefits of connecting current animals to their past lives with you. I find it lovely when I realize an animal has returned to me. You can look at them and know they loved you enough to find you again in this lifetime. It's a super affirmation that, as imperfect as we were the last time we were together, they're back. That's a good one!

And, for some of us, if we didn't do as well as we wanted the first time around, we get a chance to be better guardians this time. I enjoyed getting a chance to be a better guardian than I was the first time. I have a chance to do a better job of loving them.

For instance, when my dog Pee Wee came back as my son's dog, Peanut, I got to be her grandma and surround her with love. Even better, I was there and helped her through her transition using my animal communication and healing skills. I had a chance to make amends for my less-than stellar performance when she was Pee Wee.

If this calls to you, feel free to research reincarnation more deeply. See your life and your animal's life through the lens of reincarnation, which is all about growing through experiences. Just for fun, do a little daydreaming and invite your animals, current and past, to show you who they were in a previous lifetime. Some can be eye opening, taking you back hundreds of years ago. Some take you back to an earlier time in your current life. You never know!

I'm still gathering examples of animal reincarnation, but I'll share below a few examples to pique your interest.

〰

Mac: Is That You, Tom?

My daughter Andrea (or as I call her "Andy") rescued brother and sister kittens, Mac and Bunnie, off the streets of Richmond, Virginia, when she was in college. After graduation, Mac and Bunnie moved in with us when Andrea moved to southern India to teach English to grade-school kids.

Mac with avocados. Photo credit: Maribeth Decker.

Taking in Mac and Bunnie was such a perfect example of "what goes around comes around" in a good way. You see, I adopted Pee Wee, a street dog, while I was in the Navy, stationed in Puerto Rico. When I got orders to Japan, I didn't see how I could bring Pee Wee with me. So, I asked Mom and Dad to adopt her. And, they did!

When Mac and Bunnie came to our house, we thought we'd be finding a new home for them. We already had two dogs. Wasn't that enough? But I couldn't find anyone to adopt them as a team. They were bonded, and I didn't want to separate them. Losing Andy and then each other? Plus, my mom and dad stepped up for me and Pee Wee, so how could I say no to these little cats? I couldn't.

In my heart, I knew we'd be keeping them way before my husband

Charlie figured it out. He finally realized I couldn't let them go. They were my connection to Andy.

Here's where reincarnation comes in. I kept calling Mac "Tom," which totally confused me. I finally figured it out when I got a download that my grandmother's cat was named Tom. And then I flashed back to one of my favorite pictures: a black-and-white photo of Tom and me. I was about two years old, hunched down next to Tom with my arm around him. We were both peering intently into a ditch with a stream on my grandparent's house in West Seneca, New York.

I love that Mac is a family cat returning to me. We have such a fondness for each other as if we share this lovely memory even now.

∿

Aphrodite: More Than One Life

And then there is Aphrodite, Beverly's cat. When I did a session with Beverly and Aphrodite, there was pillow that kept drawing my eye. Beverly and Aphrodite had at least one life together somehow in the southwest United States. It was unlikely Aphrodite was a cat since, as I understand it, house cats came to America with Europeans, but I did see her as a mammal that accompanied Beverly. Maybe she was a javalina.

Aphrodite. Photo credit: Beverly.

∿

Is that you, Grandma?

Have you heard people say about a pampered animal, "Ah, I'd like to come back as a dog or cat!" Of course, they're kidding, but given the chance, maybe some do choose that life. I've met very sane people who felt like their dog was their grandfather. Some people have reported their cat has a personality exactly like their grandmother.

It may be the grandmother came back as the family cat. Or, it may be Grandmother's spirit is using the animal to let the family know she's okay. This would be with the animal's permission, of course. I think the animal feels it is doing Grandmother a favor, being of service to her and the family.

~

For those of us who believe in reincarnation, this is an interesting aspect of the relationship with our animals. I don't think it is a required belief to gain this expanded relationship, however. What is more useful is a belief that animals—and their love for us—survive death.

18

SPIRITUAL GIFTS

> When you are sorrowful look again in your heart, and you shall see that in truth you are weeping for that which has been your delight.
>
> — KHALIL GIBRAN

TO FIND LASTING comfort in spite of our animal's loss, let's remember to not focus simply on our sadness about our loss or their reasons for leaving. Their loss provides an extraordinary chance for our spiritual growth. I believe Creator offers us an awakening to spiritual knowledge we didn't possess prior to their loss.

REFLECT ON THEIR GIFTS TO YOU

When your grief has subsided a bit, think about what your animal's life and death added to your own spiritual growth.

For instance, maybe we weren't sure animals' souls survive death. Then we get a visit from them. All of a sudden, we *know* souls survive the loss of a body. And, they still love and care for us.

Maybe a sudden loss made us look at a part of our life that we were ignoring. It was time to make some changes. Maybe they made room for a new family member who needs us more than they did.

Did their leaving cause us to do some soul searching about our purpose and direction in life? Is the timing fortuitous for someone new to come into our lives, animal or human? Is there a lifestyle change we need to make? Can we see how their specific life and personality brought us gifts we couldn't see when they were alive? Did they get us through a difficult time in our lives and we've moved on?

Did your connection to your animals open an unexpected spiritual path? How has your life been enriched by their presence? How did their life prod you to improve yourself and to improve your relationship with others? Who were they asking you to be for them and for the rest of the world?

What positive character traits have been strengthened by their presence? Maybe they taught you to look for joy and delight in the moment. Or, maybe you learned patience as you worked through a tough situation.

WHAT GIFTS DID YOU BRING?

Once you've thought about the gift they brought to your life, maybe you can move on to understanding how you were the gift in their life. When you feel more peace, ask them what they received from their time with you. Expect a positive response of joy and upliftment. Did they learn to trust humans again? Maybe you loved them for who they were rather than what income they could bring into the family.

If you hear criticism or negative doubts, that's the part of you that is stuck in loss. That's not your animal's soul speaking. So, hug your still-sad self and ask again with hopeful expectation.

If their time seemed cut short—they died young or in an accident —remember that animals can achieve their spiritual goal in the twinkling of an eye. In that short time with you, what gift did they receive from you? Hold that knowledge close as you recover from your grief.

ASK FORGIVENESS FROM OUR ANIMALS

Sometimes we need to apologize and ask for forgiveness for our short-comings as their guardian. It's never too late to apologize to our animals since their spirits survive death. Asking for forgiveness from our animals assumes we have done something we wish we hadn't (or didn't do something we wish we had done). Right and wrong, it's a moral concept. That's a vulnerable spot to be in.

I don't see much asking forgiveness in the human-to-human department. But, humans asking non-humans for forgiveness? Even less frequent. Do animals have the right to expect some level of acceptable behavior from humans? That's even less common! But our animals—and all animals—deserve and have the right to some level of acceptable behavior from humans.

Does asking for forgiveness matter? It does when we understand that we can harm other beings, intentionally or unintentionally. We can decide to apologize or make amends when we haven't met our own standards of conduct.

We know animals feel, and they clearly have a consciousness, plus desires, and emotions. Scientists designed a study to confirm that even fish feel pain.[58] Guess that's because fish aren't cuddly, so we had to make sure. I hate to think how they figured out how fish felt pain. I doubt they asked an animal communicator to interview a statistically significant number of fish and report back.

If you understand that animals have their own consciousness, then there's a reason to treat them with respect and kindness, and learn to accept their peculiarities, personalities, and preferences. What you do affects the quality of their life.

We could expand this thinking to all animals, and many of us do. But let's start locally—with our own animals.

Why would we need forgiveness? We love our animals! Let's face it, sometimes our animals rub us the wrong way. We may get frustrated and angry with them. We feel embarrassed because their behaviors don't meet human standards—dogs sniff butts on a regular basis, and even humans' privates, for goodness' sakes. They bark, and then they bark some more. Cats enjoy the thrill of clawing our favorite sofa, sometimes right in front of us!

Our reactions are not always stellar. Reactions might include yelling, name calling, swatting, hitting, grabbing, kicking, yanking, locking in small spaces for too long, refusing to feed them, or withholding affection. Some of us have done these things or thought about doing them.

For instance, I bought a collar that would shock my dog, Eddy, when she barked. I was tired of her barking and I was told it would stop her. My son Pat tried the collar on himself. (If you know Pat, you're not surprised at this!) He yelled loud to set it off. Then he swore because it *really* hurt. I realized if I wouldn't use it on my kids, I shouldn't use it on Eddy. It didn't feel right. I apologized to Eddy and worked on my patience.

Maybe there's a realization that we'd neglected their physical or emotional needs. We sometimes don't understand the size of the responsibility we've taken on when we bring an animal into our household. We don't notice what they need, even though who else is going to? It's on our shoulders. When we realize we could have done better, we can take stock.

I've been guilty of "wallowing in guilt" over actions that didn't live up to my standards of care for my animals. The trouble is, humans believe wallowing in guilt is enough. There's a strange belief that if we punish ourselves emotionally with the guilt, if we bathe in the guilt, we've fixed the problem. No, that is self-centered ego, pure and simple.

Remorse is centered more on the wronged soul whereas guilt is focused on how we feel. Remorse is useful as it leads to useful thoughts, even if it's after our animal has passed.

How do we process our remorse? First, decide if you want to do better in the future. Hopefully, that's a yes! Ask yourself questions like these and formulate an action plan, even if it's only in your head:

- What was the problem exactly?
- How did it manifest?

- How much was me and how much was my animal?
- How can I make this situation better if I face it with my next animal?
- What did my animal need from me that I wasn't able to give?
- Who can I enlist to help me if it occurs again?

Remember to check your attitude and emotions. If you're stuck in anger and frustration, write your animal a love letter first so you can remember what you find delightful about them, so you can start feeling the love and affection again. Practice bringing that love and affection into your life more often.

Then apologize out loud to them when you're ready—yes, even though they've moved on in spirit. Tell them how you think you screwed up and how much you love them. Tell them how you're doing things differently with your current animals. Ask them to be a positive force in your life.

I made amends to my dog, Pee Wee, after she passed on. As you learned earlier in this book, she was my companion while I was stationed in Puerto Rico. Pee Wee was a street dog our Navy Chaplain gave to me hoping that she might help fill the need that my drinking was trying to fill. (Not recommended, by the way, but his heart was in the right place.) I was a neglectful guardian. Nothing that would scream "abuse," but it wasn't what I'd consider good caretaking as I look back.

After I got sober, I felt truly guilty about my neglect of Pee Wee. I was filled with remorse. So, I made amends to Pee Wee and promised to do better with the next animals we adopted. I got the chance to do better when we adopted two street dogs (called "poi dogs") when we lived in Hawaii. Timmie and Missy had much better lives because of my commitment to do better that time around.

Apologizing to Pee Wee was good for my soul, and, even in the afterlife, Pee Wee understood my sincerity and love. Plus, she chose to reincarnate as my son's dog, Peanut. So, I had the chance to keep my promise and be a good grandparent in the flesh with Peanut.

19

CHOOSING YOUR NEXT ANIMAL COMPANION

66 There is no remedy to love but to love more.

— HENRY DAVID THOREAU

I WANT to share a few ways to choose your next animal companion as your grief starts to abate. This is a bit different than the excellent advice given by animal rescues and shelters.[59] Let's focus on bringing a new soul into your family, not just a species or breed.

Tune into your intuitive side, especially if you've recently lost a non-human family member. This can help you focus beyond your grief to finding whoever is waiting to join you.

1. GIVE YOURSELF PERMISSION TO WAIT UNTIL YOU'RE READY

When you tell some people about your loss, these people (with the utmost love) advise you to choose a new animal *now* to help you fix your grief. But, grief is not fixed by this act. Grief has its own agenda and timing. You can certainly nudge it towards a place where it doesn't hurt as much, where there's a scar instead of an open wound.

Shutting down grief by choosing another companion isn't ideal. It's like trying to get a moody teenager who's bigger than you to go somewhere they don't want to. It takes a ton of energy, and it makes everything worse. (I take this from a personal example with my son who is now an incredibly functional adult. Hah!)

There are always repercussions with shutting down grief before it's ready. Grief comes back with a double whammy when you're not looking, almost as payback for moving forward too quickly.

Also, by waiting, you're doing your new family member a service, believe me. It's going to be hard not to compare this new soul—who has their own personality, peculiarities, and preferences—to the one you lost. And, it's doubly hard if you weren't ready to choose another animal. That's not fair to your new family member.

Thank that person for their concern and give yourself permission to hold off until you're ready to take on a new live animal project.

2. GET CONSENSUS WITH OTHER HUMANS IN THE FAMILY

Remember, they're also grieving (at least, I hope so!). They must be ready, too. When you're ready to choose a new companion, don't be the person I'm talking about in #1. Don't push other family members to move forward faster than they want.

Be kind and let them feel their grief. Maybe you can create a memorial for the animal who passed to help them (and you) understand you're not trying to replace anyone. People do that all the time.

3. TALK TO THE NON-HUMAN ANIMALS

When the humans in the family are ready to choose another animal companion, pretend you're an animal communicator. Truthfully, your animals understand more than you think. They're already tuned into your energy.

Begin here: Connect to them through your heart using the Energetic Green Smoothie. Consciously remember the love you have for them before you try to talk to them. Your feeling of love turns up the volume of your communication.

Now, talk to them out loud. Explain that it's time to bring a new soul into the house. If you have an idea of the kind of animal and their age or size, create a picture in your mind. Is it a puppy or kitten? Is it a young animal or older?

Warn them it's going to be crazy energy for a while. That's because everyone will be figuring out how to get along and learn each other's ways.

4.ASK YOUR RECENTLY DECEASED ANIMAL TO HELP

I bet they would love to help you find your next animal companion. Let them play matchmaker because they know who you need, maybe better than you do. Ask them to bring you and your next animal together in such a way that you "just know" they picked them out for you!

5. SEND OUT THE CALL "I'M READY FOR YOU!"

Pretend you're filling out a form for the energetic animal companion version of Match.com. This will help you find the right animal companion. How?

In my world, animals are part of our soul family. That's the group of souls who choose to move through life together. If you believe in reincarnation, they're the ones that were with you before you arrived on the planet, and plan on being with you in the afterlife or next life.

Have fun. Image you're a radio station broadcasting that it's time for just the right soul to come into your life now. Imagine non-human animals who are part of your soul family are tuned in and getting the message. Do it playfully, because the energy of playfulness is so attractive.

6. LOOK FOR THEM

Turn up the volume on your intuitive receiver. In other words, use your imagination.

Remember imagination? Did you ever read a story or watch a movie, and imagine being one of the characters in that story? Or, dreamed what it would be like to be a superhero or detective? Remember when you created a masterpiece with clay or crayons? How about when you talked to your cat, fish, dog, sheep, bird, or horse, and knew they understood you?

Can you find that little boy or girl, and ask them to help you out here? Send out the message: We're ready for you! We're going to be looking!

As you start your search, imagine you will just know they're the one. And, know they choose you, too. For instance, you look at picture after picture of dogs your husband sends you for adoption. All of a sudden, you see "the one." That's how we adopted my dog Tibor in 2012.

Or, you wanted to adopt them, but someone got there first. Umm, until the shelter or rescue calls a few days later. Something went haywire with the adopter and your favorite animal is back up for adoption. Somehow, they're now yours!

Or, you have doubts, so you leave to think about it. Then you return days or weeks later, and there they are, waiting for you. You know it was meant to be.

Folks have shared with me how they spent time with a roomful of puppies playing with each other, but this little girl puppy wouldn't leave them alone. They got the message. She's now part of their family.

Don't be Mr. or Ms. Logical when you're ready to choose your animal companion. Look for the serendipitous connection and do it!

Post Script: This does *not* mean the relationship will be a bed of dog or cat treats! Have you ever had a perfect human relationship? There will be bumps in the road, maybe big ones. However long they're with you, though, you were meant to be together in this time and place.

20

HONOR OTHER ANIMALS
WHO'VE PASSED

> Only if we understand, will we care. Only if we care, will
> we help. Only if we help, shall all be saved.

— JANE GOODALL

I INVITE you to honor animals who've passed even if you didn't have
a personal relationship with them. Honoring these animals connects
you and grounds you to the planet, to Mother Earth/Gaia, and her
inhabitants. Also, this practice will pull you out of your mind and back
into your heart. We need to offer more heart-centered actions to those
we cohabitate with. I'd like to offer some ideas and actions I've discovered. Let your heart guide you to the actions that resonate and bring
more joy and tenderness into the vibration of the planet. All of us,
both men and women, are invited to access our version of openheart-
edness that will help all the inhabitants of the earth thrive during
their time on this planet.

MEALTIME

I grew up saying grace with my family, thanking God for the food we were about to eat. What a wonderful habit instilled by my mother. Gratitude is such a wonderful way to start a meal!

As a vegetarian, I don't eat meals made from animals. (It felt like a conflict of interest to eat the beings whom I communicate with on a regular basis.) It's been a gradual shift. I ate seafood for quite a while. Believe it or not, a fish came into my consciousness, and said, "Why are you still eating us, Maribeth? How are we different from land animals?" I had no good answer, so I stopped eating them. I'm working on going completely plant based.

If animals or animal products are part of your meal, consider thanking them for giving you sustenance as well as thanking Creator for this food. My husband (a meat eater) and I do this at every meal. Acknowledge their contribution in this small, but powerful way. If you like, include the veggies, farmers, truckers, and all the humans who got food to us. Always definitely thank the animals, though!

Since my dogs and cats aren't vegetarians, I make it a habit to thank the animals who provided them sustenance. I am grateful for their gift of life.

HELPING DEAD ANIMALS WE DRIVE PAST

When I saw the remains of a dead animal while driving, I felt sadness and horror for their death. I thought about how those emotions don't help us or them. So, I came up with a different strategy, which I'd like to share with you.

When you see the remains of the animal, reach out to their spirit and ask them if they're okay. Seriously, just do it and don't worry if it's real. It will work.

You might hear, "Yes, I'm fine!" You then may feel a bit of gratitude for being asked! You can continue on your trip, knowing all is well with them.

If you feel their panic as if they're still stuck in those last moments, send soft love. Tell them to move up and out of their body. Imagine there's a small cohort of friends and family to greet them and bring them across the Rainbow Bridge. Feel their relief—and yours. You did a good deed!!

Or maybe you just feel someone's presence! Every so often, I connect with ("run into" seems a good analogy) animals who are still attached to our world instead of transitioning into the next world. A term used in a lot of shows about hauntings call them ghosts. It's a useful term except it makes them scarier than most of them are.

I think ghost stories are fun to read, but I don't think it's beneficial for the animal (or a human) to be stuck on the planet after they've left their body. So, if I feel an animal's presence, I let them know that they don't have to stay here. I tell the animal there's a better place to be, to enjoy life again. They don't need to stay here.

I invite members of their species who are good at transitions and care about this soul. Picture family coming forward to greet and welcome them. Sometimes I ask the animal to look for light beings. Look for the brightest, most beautiful energies and go with them to the brightest, highest light they can get to. I imagine that I'm watching them go. You could do this, too. If they say thank you, be sure to respond.

Again, if you have heard about a tragedy of some kind, imagine you're tapping into the animals that have passed. Ask if you can help them move up so they feel better. Tell them to move to the highest light they can find, and again picture someone waiting for them, ready to help them recover. Reassure them that if it feels like a soft, comforting, loving light, they can relax and move towards it. Feel them rise and find a safe place surrounded with love. Wish them well.

If you find a small dead animal on your walks (relatively intact and you're not squeamish), bury it. Or, move it back to the earth if it's on the sidewalk/road and cover it with leaves. Bless it or say a short prayer so it feels cared for.

And, so you know, the animals I have talked about in this book have moved on; they are not stuck on earth. They can visit us or communicate with us, and they are clear about the fact they have transitioned.

ALLOW WILD ANIMALS TO THRIVE SO WE DON'T HAVE TO MOURN THEIR EXTINCTION

Lately, I've been drawn to considering what our world will be like if more animals find their habitats uninhabitable. In 1962, when DDT was endangering birds everywhere, Rachel Carson wrote *Silent Spring*, explaining how DDT was so dangerous. A more recent movie, *Avengers: Endgame* gave us a visual picture of what the earth might be like if fifty percent of living beings were taken away from the planet. Hearing birds sing again at the end of the movie was such a wonderful feeling.

And I've even had messages from my totem animals that they're concerned about the state of the world, too. I'd like to share a blog post I wrote so that you will consider joining me in caring for the health of the world for all our animals.

On the same Sunday, a turtle, a bear (via video), and a fox strolled into my life. Since they are my top three totem animals,[60] I had to see what the message from the Universe was. Here's how it unfolded.

I met the box turtle on a path in Fort Hunt Park in Virginia. It was my usual Sunday morning walk with doggies, Tibor and Stella. This turtle didn't box itself in. Instead, it just sat there and looked at me. I walked Tibor and Stella gingerly around it. As I passed, I caressed it on its back and said, "Nice to see you!" And, I meant it.

Later that day, I was working on this second edition you're reading right now. I nudged the computer mouse by mistake and a story popped up that stopped me in my tracks. It showed me a video of a black bear strolling down the aisle of a Ralph's grocery store in Porter Ranch, California. I'm sure she was looking for honey!

Finally, around 10 p.m. on that Sunday night, I took the dogs for their final walk. We didn't go far because Stella had trouble walking, but she was still up for the walk as long as she got to pee and sniff!

I heard a cry that sounded like ... a cat howling in distress...a dog yelping in distress...an upset toddler...*a fox!*

It was in the grassy area on the other side of the Mount Vernon House. I hadn't seen a fox in our area for a couple years, so we walked over to see if we could find her. We did! As I saw her, I whistled to get her attention and said, "Hi!" She turned her head, looked at us, and we all stopped for a bit. Then we all went on our way.

It wasn't until the next day that I realized this couldn't be a coincidence! Three totem animals in one day? I believe this message is for all of us, not just me, and it applies whenever you read this. That's the lovely secret of gifts from Creator: They have no expiration date.

I'd been crying inconsolably off and on for a month. Try not to judge me too harshly.

My crying was the kind that overtook me with deep, gulping sobs —the kind of sobs that come unannounced when you lose someone very close: a partner, parent, child, good friend or beloved animal companion.

I told my husband Charlie. Of course, being the logical guy he is, Charlie asked the logical question, "Have you checked in with all the humans you love?" Good idea! I talked to my kids, my sister's kids (niece and nephew), Debbie, and Aunt Norma in Buffalo. Being me, I also checked in with my older dogs and cats (I have four) to see if they were nearing the end of their life. Nothing explained my grief—until the 2021 Climate Change Report.

Coincidentally, the Intergovernmental Panel on Climate Change (IPCC) issued its sixth report on the health of the natural world in 2021. When my husband, who is my personal news reporter told me, he explained, "Basically, we're f***ed." (He's a sailor, okay?)

I cried as if someone I loved had died, and I finally understood the message. I was mourning that Earth is having trouble sustaining our lives. This is the first paragraph of the World Resources Institute's 5 Big Findings from the IPCC's 2021 Climate Report:

Headlines related to recent extreme weather appear to come out of a science fiction book: Even the richest countries in the world can't control widespread fires — they're even burning in the Arctic. Deadly flooding in Germany and Belgium in July 2021 completely washed away buildings and cars, and more than 1,000 people remain missing. Hundreds died in flooding in China. The U.S. Pacific Northwest, known for its cool climate, hit over 100 degrees F for several days. And the Arctic lost an area of sea ice equivalent to the size of Florida between June and mid-July 2021.[61]

I'm old enough to remember this scene in the great 1967 movie *The Graduate*. Sadly, I feel the irony deep in my DNA as the savvy businessman gives his best advice to the college graduate to move into plastics because it was going to be big business. And, yes, plastics contribute to global warming.

For a spiritual perspective, I opened Henri J.M. Nouwen's book, *Life of the Beloved, Spiritual Living in a Secular World*, written in the mid-90s, and found this staring at me:

I notice in myself how often my body is tense, how I usually keep my guard up and how seldom I have a complete feeling of being at home. If I then turn to the Toronto suburbs where I live and see the pretentious mega-houses, the ugly shopping malls strewn about to make consumption more efficient and the alluring billboards promising comfort and relaxation in very seductive ways – all of that while forests are demolished, streams dried up, deer and rabbits and birds driven out of my environment – I am not surprised that my body screams for a healing touch and reassuring embrace."[62]

My totem animals asked how we humans will cherish the gift we've been given—this planet and all its inhabitants. More specifically, they'd like us to reconsider who we are individually and our impact as a species. Here's what I heard from them:

When we came into your presence yesterday, Maribeth, we

reminded you there's always hope. Life asserts itself. Life will continue to assert itself. Gaia will find a way to continue. And, we non-humans want to remind you of our strong desire to continue living on this planet.

What does being human mean to your species? Are you still biological beings filled with Spirit from Creator? Or, have you finally become biological machines tied to material needs?

Life is about balance and balance will be restored. Balance will be restored.

We ask you to reclaim your connection to the natural world. Find the beauty Creator has given all of us. Remember you're a part of the natural world. Nurture yourselves through the world that exists beyond that which was created by humans. Join the other creatures of the world. Restore our world and yours.

It's not too late.

21

FINAL THOUGHTS

66 Love is not written on paper, for paper can be erased.
Nor is it etched on stone, for stone can be broken. But it
is inscribed on a heart and there it shall remain forever.

— RUMI

WHAT DO I want you to remember? Oops, I've been corrected. What
do your animals want you to remember? That they came into your life
for a purpose. That they passed when they are supposed to. That you
were the right soul for them, and they were the right soul for you at
that time in your life.

Love is an energy that is never destroyed. There are no exceptions.
A loving relationship may be transformed, but it is forever.

It's a great honor for those who have passed on to be grieved over,
to be missed. It is right to grieve for your animals. This is a gift you
give to those you love. This is a way of physically showing them and
the world they were important to you. I thank you for feeling that for
them. The humanity in you shines so brightly with your remembrance
of them.

And, if no one else has said it, thank you for caring for them until they passed. For being their family all the way to the end. For making the decision to let them go when life was no longer good for them— even when you knew how hard it was going to be without them.

Think of each animal we've loved as having a permanent connection to our soul and ours to theirs. I see the love as beams of light between our souls. Maybe we have a permanent list of animal contacts in our souls that keeps track of each one through the years and lifetimes. If this thought appeals to you, meditate on creating an image that will help you feel your connection to your animals.

If you weren't a perfect animal guardian, it is never too late to offer a sincere apology to your animal. They are willing to forgive you and let it go (and it's good for your soul). Like a real friend, they hope if there's something you can do better for the next animal, you'll do it. But, they're not hung up on it. They are pretty good at letting go once they have transitioned. They just love you.

If you feel relief after an animal with chronic conditions has passed, know that they feel the same way! They're feeling, "Like wow, glad that part is over with!"

Use what I've shared to re-frame the grief and guilt you may feel about animals who have passed. Allow yourself to see and feel the deep connection and love you and your animal have for each other.

If you still feel grief or guilt, write a letter to your animal or talk to them as if they can hear you. They can. Imagine they respond to you in the kindest, most loving way. You can even imagine them as the same size as you so you can give each other a hug. Imagine whatever situation helps you be complete and close the chapter on this particular *physical* relationship. They need you to release them, give them room to figure out what's next. They have new adventures awaiting them!

Consider the possibility that reading this book might be the key to expanding your mind and connecting with your animals before, during, and after they have passed on.

Finally, please consider all the animals on the planet and what they need from us.

RESOURCES

CRYSTALS

Crystal Bible: A Definitive Guide to Crystals by Judy Hall
   Book of Stones: Who They Are and What They Teach by Robert Simmons
& Naisha Ahsia. Check out the Stone Property Reference Index for
physical and emotional issues

EUTHANASIA AT HOME

Your veterinarian may be able to provide information about vets who
provide euthanasia at home. Also check Lap of Love: http://www.
lapoflove.com/. They are a network of veterinarians around the
country.

HOMEOPATHY

Homeopathic Care for Cats & Dogs, by Don Hamilton, DMV, Revised
2010, North Atlantic Books, Berkeley, California.

HOSPICE

There doesn't seem to be a national website, so search for animal hospice services in your locale.

How Do I Know When it's Time? Assessing Quality of Life for Your Companion Animal and Making End-of-Life Decisions

This Ohio State University Veterinary Medical Center checklist (https://vet.osu.edu/vmc/sites/default/files/import/assets/pdf/ hospital/companionAnimals/HonoringtheBond/ HowDoIKnowWhen.pdf) gives you a grounded way to review your animal's quality of life. We're so darn emotional at this stage, having a neutral checklist allows us to take a step back from our emotions. It has helped me get beyond the grief to see what's best for my animal when considering whether to let them go or support them as they age.

MASSAGE

Visit Maribeth Decker's YouTube Channel at https://www.youtube. com/c/maribethdecker/ and search for massage.

QUANTUM-TOUCH®

Website https://www.quantumtouch.com/en/

Ebook, Editor Chaya Silberstein, "Everyday Miracles with Quantum-Touch: Energy Healing For Animals (Volume 1)," 2018. My healing for my Siberian Husky Mitsubishi is included in the book.

Walton, Adara L. "The Effects of Quantum-Touch® on Chronic Musculoskeletal Pain: A Pilot Study." Energy Psychology 3, no. 2 (November 2011): 25-39. doi:10.4135/9781473931312.

REINCARNATION

What groups believe in reincarnation?

- Reincarnation is an important part of Jain, Hindu, Buddhist, and Sikh religions.
- Some early Christian sects believed in reincarnation, although that hasn't survived into current Christian traditions. From https://www.near-death.com/reincarnation/history/judaism.html.
- For Judaism, research points to the mystical Jewish tradition, Kabbalah, as believing in reincarnation as well. From https://www.near-death.com/reincarnation/history/judaism.html
- Some North American tribal beliefs supporting reincarnation. See https://nativevoicesbooks.com/content/reincarnation-beliefs-north-american-indians

Animals and The Buddha https://www.youtube.com/watch?v=SOMWAAykFuc&t=21s

Time between lives: https://reincarnationafterdeath.com/how-long-does-it-take/

SENIOR PEOPLE WITH ANIMALS AND SENIOR DOGS

Coping with Losing a Pet (scroll down to "Tips for Seniors"), https://www.helpguide.org/articles/grief/coping-with-losing-a-pet.htm

ENDNOTES

1. Lewis, C. S. *A Grief Observed*. San Francisco, CA: Seabury Pr., 1961.
2. "Wave-Particle Duality." ScienceDaily. ScienceDaily. Accessed May 23, 2016. https://www.sciencedaily.com/terms/wave-particle_duality.htm.
3. Nelson, R. D., Y. H. Dobyns, B. J. Dunne, and R. G. Jahn. "GCP: Analysis of Variance of Reg Experiments." Princeton University. The Trustees of Princeton University. Accessed May 23, 2016. http://noosphere.princeton.edu/rdnelson/anova.html.
4. Zion, Tina. "Medical Intuition - Blog." Tina Zion. https://tinazion.com/medical-intuition-blog/.
5. Guthridge, Liz. "Remembering Gustav with Three Life Lessons." Connect's Creations, November 24, 2015. http://www.icontact-archive.com/pRq9-fueo_ap8Jo75u3rOZOrj-sbTK8Sn.
6. Guthridge, Liz. "3 Good Behavior Lessons from Gustav." Connect Consulting Group. https://connectconsulting-group.com/3-good-behavior-lessons-from-gustav/.

7. *A Dog Helps Stranded Motorists in Ireland. YouTube*, 2017. https://www.youtube.com/watch?v=7WS5PNlK0vY&t=7s.

8. Eveleth, Rose. "Does This Cat Know When You're Going to Die?" *Smithsonian Magazine*, September 20, 2012. https://www.smithsonianmag.com/smart-news/does-this-cat-know-when-youre-going-to-die-44969110/.

9. Schumann, John Henning. "How Super Sniffer Dogs Are Helping Detect Disease around the World." NPR. NPR, January 25, 2020. https://www.npr.org/sections/health-shots/2020/01/25/799404129/how-super-sniffer-dogs-are-helping-detect-disease-around-the-world.

10. Goodavage, Maria. *Doctor Dogs: How Our Best Friends Are Becoming Our Best Medicine*. US: E P Dutton & Co Inc, 2021.

11. Cunningham, Val. "Turns out Birds Can Smell and Taste after All." Star Tribune. Star Tribune, June 19, 2018. https://www.startribune.com/turns-out-birds-can-smell-and-taste-after-all/485946142/.

12. "Hachikō." Wikipedia. Wikimedia Foundation, May 23, 2016. https://en.wikipedia.org/wiki/Hachik%C5%8D.

13. Pleasance, Chris Pleasance. "German Shepherd Has Stood by Owner's Grave for 10 Years." Daily Mail Online. Associated Newspapers, August 16, 2017. https://www.dailymail.co.uk/news/article-4795318/German-shepherd-stood-owner-s-grave-10-years.html.

14. Johnson, Ben. "The Story of Greyfriars Bobby." Historic UK. Accessed February 25, 2022. https://www.historic-uk.com/HistoryUK/HistoryofScotland/Greyfriars-Bobby/.

15. Simpson, William E. "How Wild Horses Deal with Death and Grief: A Rare Insight." Horsetalk.co.nz, July 9, 2018. https://www.horsetalk.co.nz/2018/07/04/wild-horses-death-grief-insight/.

16. Briggs, Chelsi. "Animal-Assisted Healing and Pain Management." Pain Management and Injury Relief, August 19, 2015. http://paininjuryrelief.com/animal-assisted-healing-and-pain-management/.

17. Casciotti, Dana, and Diana Zuckerman. "The Benefits of
    Pets for Human Health." National Center for Health
    Research, January 14, 2014. https://www.center4re-
    search.org/benefits-pets-human-health/.
18. DeNoon, Daniel. "A Dog Could Be Your Heart's Best
    Friend." Harvard Health, May 22, 2013.
    http://www.health.harvard.edu/blog/a-dog-could-be-your-
    hearts-best-friend-201305226291.
19. Rovner, Julie. "Pet Therapy: How Animals and Humans Heal
    Each Other." NPR. NPR, March 5, 2012. http://www.n-
    pr.org/sections/health-shots/2012/03/09/146583986/pet-
    therapy-how-animals-and-humans-heal-each-other.
20. Grant, Robert J. *The Place We Call Home: Exploring the Soul's
    Existence after Death*. Virginia Beach, VA: A.R.E. Press, 2000.
21. *Monty Python and the Holy Grail. IMDb*. IMDb.com, 1975.
    https://www.imdb.com/title/tt0071853/.
22. "Stress Effects on the Body." American Psychological
    Association. American Psychological Association, November
    1, 2018. https://www.apa.org/topics/stress/body.
23. Fox, Michael W. *The Healing Touch for Cats: The Proven Massage
    Program*. New York, NY: Newmarket Press, 2004.
24. Fox, Michael W. *The Healing Touch for Dogs*. New York, NY:
    Newmarket, 2004.
25. Tellington TTouch Worldwide. "Research & Studies."
    Tellington TTouch Training®. Tellington TTouch Worldwide,
    June 11, 2021. https://ttouch.com/About_Us/Re-
    search_Studies/index.html.
26. Silva, Nuno E O F, Stelio P L Luna, Jean G F Joaquim,
    Heloisa D Coutinho, and Fábio S Possebon. "Effect of
    Acupuncture on Pain and Quality of Life in Canine
    Neurological and Musculoskeletal Diseases." The Canadian
    veterinary journal = La revue veterinaire canadienne.
    Canadian Veterinary Medical Association, September 2017.
    https://www.ncbi.nlm.nih.gov/pmc/articles/PMC5556488/.
27. Huisheng, Xie. "How to Use Acupuncture to Treat Renal

Failure," Powered By VIN, 2011.https://www.vin.com/ap-
putil/content/defaultadv1.aspx?pId=11343&meta=gener-
ic&catId=34551&id=5124189&ind=7&objTypeID=17.

28. Parnell. "Osteoarthritis in Dogs - Signs and Treatment."
American Kennel Club. American Kennel Club, June 22,
2021. https://www.akc.org/expert-advice/health/os-
teoarthritis-signs-treatment/.

29. "Chronic Kidney Disease." Cornell University College of
Veterinary Medicine, March 1, 2019. https://www.vet.cor-
nell.edu/departments-centers-and-institutes/cornell-feline-
health-center/health-information/feline-health-
topics/chronic-kidney-disease.

30. Decker, Maribeth. "Acupuncture for Dog Nausea." Web log.
Sacred Grove (blog), n.d. https://sacredgrove.-
com/acupressure-for-dog-nausea/.

31. Cuno, Charles. "Canine Anxiety & Stomach Chi." Tallgrass
Animal Acupressure Resources, August 24, 2016.
https://www.animalacupressure.com/blogs/animal-
acupressure/canine-anxiety-stomach-chi-animal-
acupressure.

32. Snow. "Acupressure for Your Dog's Stomach." Animal
Wellness Magazine, September 7, 2018. https://animalwell-
nessmagazine.com/acupressure-dog-stomach/.

33. Snow, Amy, and Nancy Zidonis. "Acupressure Can Relieve
Nausea." Whole Dog Journal, May 1, 2020.
https://www.whole-dog-journal.com/care/acupressure-can-
relieve-nausea/.

34. Snow, Amy, and Nancy Zidonis. "Enhancing Feline
Digestion with Acupressure." Tallgrass Animal Acupressure
Resources, November 16, 2016. https://www.animalacu-
pressure.com/blogs/animal-acupressure/enhancing-feline-
digestion-with-acupressure.

35. Decker, Maribeth. "When Your Cat Won't Eat." Web log.
Sacred Grove (blog), n.d. https://sacredgrove.com/when-
your-cat-wont-eat/ .

36. Decker, Maribeth. "Acupressure for Dog Nausea." Web log. *Sacred Grove* (blog), n.d. https://sacredgrove.-com/acupressure-for-dog-nausea/.

37. Tenny, Susan. *Canine Relaxation Heart 1. Www.ElementalAcu-pressure.com.* Susan Tenny, n.d. https://youtu.be/eI8tr6axrlQ.

38. Dima, R., Francio V. Tieppo, C. Towery, and S. Davani. "Review of Literature on Low-Level Laser Therapy Benefits for Nonpharmacological Pain Control in Chronic Pain and Osteoarthritis." Alternative therapies in health and medicine. U.S. National Library of Medicine. https://pubmed.ncbi.nlm.nih.gov/28987080/.

39. "What Is Veterinary Laser Therapy?" America Animal Hospital Association. https://www.aaha.org/your-pet/pet-owner-education/ask-aaha/laser-therapy/.

40. Bone, Kerry, and Simon Y. Mills. *Principles and Practice of Phytotherapy.* Edinburgh, Scotland: Churchill Livingstone, 2000.

41. Shurkin, Joel. "News Feature: Animals That Self-Medicate." Proceedings of the National Academy of Sciences of the United States of America. National Academy of Sciences, December 9, 2014. https://www.ncbi.nlm.nih.-gov/pmc/articles/PMC4267359/.

42. Tuttle, Debbie. *Wealthy in the Woods,* 2018.

43. Nazzaro, Filomena, Florinda Fratianni, Laura De Martino, Raffaele Coppola, and Vincenzo De Feo. "Effect of Essential Oils on Pathogenic Bacteria." Pharmaceuticals (Basel, Switzerland). MDPI, November 25, 2013. https://www.ncbi.nlm.nih.gov/pmc/articles/PMC3873673/.

44. Chen, Weiyang, Ilze Vermaak, and Alvaro Viljoen. "Camphor--a Fumigant during the Black Death and a Coveted Fragrant Wood in Ancient Egypt and Babylon--a Review." Molecules (Basel, Switzerland). MDPI, May 10, 2013. https://www.ncbi.nlm.nih.gov/pmc/articles/PMC6270224/.

45. "Essential Oils and Horses." Web log. *Plant Therapy* (blog).

Everyday Essentials, April 13, 2019. https://blog.planttthera-
py.com/blog/2019/04/13/essential-oils-and-horses/.

46. Decker, Maribeth. "Confessions of a Terrible Pet Parent."
    Web log. *Sacred Grove* (blog), n.d. https://sacredgrove.-
    com/confessions-of-a-terrible-pet-parent/.

47. Sollars, David. *The Complete Idiot's Guide to Homeopathy.*
    Indianapolis, IN: Alpha, 2001.

48. Decker, Maribeth. "Healing Our Animals with Crystals."
    Web log. *Sacred Grove* (blog), n.d. https://sacredgrove.-
    com/healing-our-animals-with-crystals/.

49. "Gemstone Toxicity Table - International Gem Society -
    IGS." International Gem Society, January 18, 2022.
    https://www.gemsociety.org/article/gemstone-toxicity-
    table/.

50. Lama, Zen. "The 7 Chakras - A Beginners Guide to Your
    Energy System." Zenlama, May 24, 2018. https://www.zen-
    lama.com/the-7-chakras-a-beginners-guide-to-your-energy-
    system/.

51. *The Energetic Green Smoothie. YouTube.* Sacred Grove with
    Maribeth Decker, n.d. https://www.youtube.com/watch?
    v=4wRsq43fnmQ.

52. Gordon, Richard. *Quantum-Touch: the Power to Heal.* Berkeley,
    CA: North Atlantic Books, 2006.

53. Dodman, Nicholas. "Helping Your 'Good Old Dog' Navigate
    Aging." NPR. NPR, November 23, 2010. https://www.n-
    pr.org/2010/11/23/131516152/helping-your-good-old-dog-
    navigate-aging.

54. Decker, Maribeth. "Bird Talk with Erin Doherty." Web log.
    Sacred Grove (blog), n.d. https://sacredgrove.com/bird-talk-
    with-erin-doherty/.

55. Robinson, Lawrence. "Coping with Losing a Pet."
    HelpGuide.org, February 8, 2022.
    https://www.helpguide.org/articles/grief/coping-with-
    losing-a-pet.htm.

56. Ball, Alyssa. "What to Do When You Can't Take Care of

Your Pet Anymore." Looking for Senior Home Care? Caring Senior Service. https://www.caringseniorservice.com/blog/take-care-of-pets.

57. Semkiw, Walter. "Do We Reincarnate as Animals? Telepathy with Animals and the Unified Field of Consciousness." Reincarnation Research, July 31, 2021. https://www.reincarnationresearch.com/do-we-reincarnate-as-animals-telepathy-with-animals/.

58. Jabr, Faris. "It's Official: Fish Feel Pain." Smithsonian.com. Smithsonian Institution, January 8, 2018. https://www.smithsonianmag.com/science-nature/fish-feel-pain-180967764/.

59. "Adopting from an Animal Shelter or Rescue Group." The Humane Society of the United States. https://www.humanesociety.org/resources/adopting-animal-shelter-or-rescue-group.

60. Beauchesne, Myriam. "The Origination of the Spirit Animal." Kheops International, December 20, 2018. https://kheopsinternational.com/blog/origination-of-the-spirit-animal/.

61. "International Panel on Climate Change 2021: The Physical Science Basis." Sixth Assessment Report. Accessed February 25, 2022. https://www.ipcc.ch/report/ar6/wg1/.

62. Nouwen, Henri J.M. *Life of the Beloved: Spiritual Living in a Secular World.* New York, NY: Crossroad Pub. Co., 1993.

ORIGINAL FOREWORD

Peace in Passing addresses in-depth your ultimate question: "is there life after death?" The resounding answer is *"Yes."*

But my bet is that you knew that already. That's why you're reading this book right now.

Regardless of your motivation for reading this book however, I'm honored to be the first to wholeheartedly congratulate you, because by opening this magical work you have just taken one powerful step on the journey to your soul's expansion and healing in this lifetime.

Let me assure you, by the way, that you have picked the right tour guide for exploring the afterlife. Maribeth Decker is just what the doctor ordered for where you're at – she's a gentle, down to earth, compassionate and exceptionally talented guide to masterfully nudge you along this juncture in your life's spiritual journey.

Now, as a natural intuitive, I am quite aware of how few people can understand, converse with and respect our animal family – I myself have been seeing and conversing with my dear deceased tuxedo cat Puff who was with me for the first 21 years of my life for many years now. Her shadow still appears from time to time about my home, and whenever I am anxious, I see visions of her and feel her warm, loving presence near me.

Because of Puff's steady presence throughout my life, animal and spirit communication is quite normal, even mundane to me. Yet I learned the hard way that this is not normal or mundane for everyone, so when I venture to share or comment on a message coming from a transitioned loved one or animal with a regular person who may not share my natural sensitivity, they usually respond with dismissive and confused looks, or better yet they may freak out or say I'm "crazy" for saying such things. Perhaps you can relate?

Most people are socialized to frown on or avoid paranormal and otherworldly experiences, and this socialization can make those of us who are more sensitive – or who have been forced into sensitization through profound grief or a traumatic event – to feel like we are "crazy" outsiders, that we're being "unreasonable" or just plain silly.

This contemporary ignorance breeds disrespect and alienation. What's worse is that it adds insult to injury for those of us who are processing grieving the loss of our beloved pet. What if we just want to say goodbye? Or what if we want to know if they are alright, wherever they are? Is that so wrong or "silly" to ask? Certainly not.

You're not crazy. You're human. And this book is meant to honor you and your truth.

So I must say how incredibly grateful and in awe I am of Maribeth's love offering to our human family with the creation of this book, because as we understand the art of animal communication and transition, we humans get to learn just how we are deeply connected to our Earth – we are all part of Nature.

I believe this is truly a healing book. As you read the pages, notice how your energy responds. It is meant to heal you and has been infused with healing energy for you.

Through sharing story after story of various animal families' preparations for transition, transition ceremonies and afterlife communications, Maribeth's research and down-to-earth guidance definitively shows and validates something you already knew:

Love never dies.

So whether you've picked up this book out of anger or idle curiosity, whether you've opened these pages to assuage your grief or suspicion, or whether you're seeking confirmation of the reality of that supernatural event which you've experienced already, please know this: you are seen, heard, and never alone – these three things all of our animal family intuitively teaches us already.

But I invite you to check your disbelief at the door, because in these precious pages you'll embark on a sacred journey behind the veil, beyond one of life's biggest mysteries: death and the hereafter.

Know that the following stories will not only open your heart to the profound dignity and power of your beloved pets' transitioning from a state of being alive to – what Puff has told me to say is, "more than alive", but also know that as you read on, you'll experience comfort, courage and healing for your own human experience of death as well.

Dealing with death is indeed frightening and painful, but with the right mindset, as Maribeth so candidly shares and exemplifies here, we can begin to access the unique brilliance of how our spiritual soul-family ties are unbreakable and continue on, no matter what.

Take a moment to consider the implications of this...

Breathe deeply.

I pray that as you move from page to page, you find that which you seek: peace in passing.

In deep love and service,
Sensei Victoria Whitfield
Internationally recognized natural intuition expert, speaker and spiritual teacher

ABOUT THE AUTHOR

 Maribeth Decker is the founder of Sacred-Grove.com—*Where People and Pets Heal and Connect.* She works with animal guardians who dearly love their animal and yet are facing tough animal issues. She uses her intuitive animal communication, medical intuition, and energetic healing skills to address animals' physical, emotional, and behavioral issues. Maribeth's mission is to bring a greater depth of love, compassion, and comfort into the human-animal relationship.

Her rich personal life experiences have enabled her to bring a wealth of heart-centered wisdom to her work with each client. Her unyielding intention is to consistently bring forth the maximum benefit for all concerned in the most benevolent manner possible.

Maribeth lives near the Potomac River in Alexandria, Virginia, with her husband, Charlie; dogs, Stella and Tibor; and cats, Mac, Bunnie, and Shadow.

 facebook.com/sacredgrovepets
instagram.com/maribethdecker
youtube.com/maribethdecker

ABOUT THE PUBLISHER

Highlander Press, founded in 2019, is a mid-sized publishing company committed to sharing big ideas and changing the world through words.

Highlander Press guides authors through the publishing, launching, and promoting process and beyond, focusing on ensuring they have impactful books of which they are proud, making a long-time dream come true. Having authored a book improves confidence, creates clarity, and ensures that your story and expertise are available to those who need them.

What makes Highlander Press unique is its business model focuses on building strong, collaborative relationships with other women-owned businesses, which specialize in some aspect of the publishing industry, such as graphic design, book marketing, book launching, copyrights, and publicity. The mantra "a rising tide lifts all boats" is one they embrace. You can find their latest publications and submission guidelines at https://highlanderpressbooks.com.

facebook.com/highlanderpress
instagram.com/highlanderpress
linkedin.com/highlanderpress

Made in the USA
Las Vegas, NV
28 April 2022